Cambridge Elements

Elements in the Global Middle Ages
edited by
Geraldine Heng
University of Texas at Austin
Susan J. Noakes
University of Minnesota–Twin Cities
Lynn Ramey
Vanderbilt University

GLOBAL SHIPS

Seafaring, Shipwrecks, and Boatbuilding in the Global Middle Ages

Amanda Respess
The Ohio State University-Marion

CAMBRIDGE
UNIVERSITY PRESS

Shaftesbury Road, Cambridge CB2 8EA, United Kingdom

One Liberty Plaza, 20th Floor, New York, NY 10006, USA

477 Williamstown Road, Port Melbourne, VIC 3207, Australia

314–321, 3rd Floor, Plot 3, Splendor Forum, Jasola District Centre, New Delhi – 110025, India

103 Penang Road, #05–06/07, Visioncrest Commercial, Singapore 238467

Cambridge University Press is part of Cambridge University Press & Assessment, a department of the University of Cambridge.

We share the University's mission to contribute to society through the pursuit of education, learning and research at the highest international levels of excellence.

www.cambridge.org
Information on this title: www.cambridge.org/9781009494373

DOI: 10.1017/9781009343411

© Amanda Respess 2024

This publication is in copyright. Subject to statutory exception and to the provisions of relevant collective licensing agreements, no reproduction of any part may take place without the written permission of Cambridge University Press & Assessment.

When citing this work, please include a reference to the DOI 10.1017/9781009343411

First published 2024

A catalogue record for this publication is available from the British Library.

ISBN 978-1-009-49437-3 Hardback
ISBN 978-1-009-34339-8 Paperback
ISSN 2632-3427 (online)
ISSN 2632-3419 (print)

Cambridge University Press & Assessment has no responsibility for the persistence or accuracy of URLs for external or third-party internet websites referred to in this publication and does not guarantee that any content on such websites is, or will remain, accurate or appropriate.

Global Ships

Seafaring, Shipwrecks, and Boatbuilding in the Global Middle Ages

Elements in the Global Middle Ages

DOI: 10.1017/9781009343411
First published online: November 2024

Amanda Respess
The Ohio State University-Marion

Author for correspondence: Amanda Respess, Respess.1@osu.edu

Abstract: *Global Ships* examines the major seafaring traditions and technologies that engendered long-distance connections across the world's oceans during the Global Middle Ages. Between the years 500 and 1500 CE, maritime trade networks spanning the seas globalized commodities, religions, and trade diasporas in an increasingly mobile world. Focusing on shipbuilding traditions, nautical cultures, sailing itineraries, and examples of recovered shipwrecks and cargoes from around the world, *Global Ships* provides an expert overview of the major vessels that sailed the seas in the Global Middle Ages. A concise interpretive guide to global maritime technologies and cultures for researchers, teachers, and students, *Global Ships* highlights essential historical context, technological case studies, and logics of seafaring around the world before the modern age.

Keywords: Global Middle Ages, maritime history, maritime archaeology, shipwrecks, world history

© Amanda Respess 2024

ISBNs: 9781009494373 (HB), 9781009343398 (PB), 9781009343411 (OC)
ISSNs: 2632-3427 (online), 2632-3419 (print)

Contents

Global Ships: An Introduction   1

1 A Prehistory of Boatbuilding and Long-Distance Trade Networks   7

2 Austronesian Boatbuilding and Seafaring, Southeast Asian Lashed-Lug Vessels   15

3 Sewn-Boats from the Western Indian Ocean   21

4 Hybrid Ships in China and Southeast Asia   28

5 Competition and Change in the Mediterranean   37

6 Viking Ships and Trade Vessels in Northern and Western Europe   42

7 Weaponized Ships   47

Conclusion   51

References   53

Global Ships: An Introduction

Once upon a time, when I was an undergraduate research intern at The Field Museum of Natural History in Chicago, I experienced a jolt to my preconceptions about the past while working with objects from the museum's *Java Sea Shipwreck* collection. I had been tasked, along with other students and volunteers, with the job of vetting the objects described in our archaeological reports by physically examining the many hundreds of shipwreck bowls that had come into our collections from an 800-year-old vessel. Our task was simple – to carefully look at the bowls and other ceramics one at a time, measuring them, identifying their color patterns, noting every scratch in the glaze and area where the decoration may have been eroded by centuries of hard living on the seafloor. As you routinize this process over days and weeks, it eventually becomes meditative. You look at each bowl and record its dimensions and designs, but after hours of artifact-after-artifact passing through your hands, you begin to see past the number of centimeters that comprise the diameter of an object, and the cracked-ice appearance of its broken glaze. Seeing hundreds (and thousands) of bowls and other ceramics from a single cargo allows you to suddenly see the individual bowl, the individual artifact, in a new light. When this happens, you encounter a series of surprises that only material objects from the very distant past can deliver: unexpected fingerprints left by the hands that created them, faded inscriptions that suddenly come into sharp focus, hidden drawings scribbled on the undersides of containers. These unexpected discoveries pack a powerful punch because they connect us directly with the relatable humanity of people living many centuries ago, they are a direct line to the last hands, eyes, and minds to touch these materials before they were buried underwater.

Today, when I cover the topics of global connections and trade in the premodern world in my undergraduate courses, my students typically voice a familiar echo of surprise after we begin diving into the readings and lectures about long-distance seafaring: *"Why didn't anyone tell me this before?"* It is always the same course materials that provoke this response: images and case studies of shipwreck artifacts recovered from the global trade routes. For my students, these ships and their cargoes reveal unexpected aspects of premodern relationships and daily life that defy expectations about the complexity and connectivity of the past. Specifically, they present a picture of an interconnected world that popular understandings tell them should not have existed before the voyages of Christopher Columbus. But the material evidence that is traceable through wreckage across the world's oceans makes clear that the period between 500 and 1500 CE witnessed a dramatic intensification in the scale of global seafaring that would shape the political and economic relationships of both the premodern and modern worlds. *Global Ships* explores this upsurge in long-distance maritime activity by examining the major seafaring traditions that spanned the world's oceans during the Global Middle Ages.

The purpose of this *Element* is to provide a general, introductory sketch of the material history of premodern seafaring in the Old World that is accessible to non-specialists, be they students or scholars. It is not a work of new research, but an assemblage of examples from the world's oceans that surveys key technological developments in interconnected maritime regions. To adequately historicize premodern maritime technology, even at the introductory level found in *Global Ships*, it is also necessary to explicitly discuss the role that seafaring and technology have played in the political and cultural imaginaries of Western historiography. This text is intended for use in the classroom or by political and cultural historians whose work draws them to the findings of maritime archaeology and who require a concise overview of the significance of extant premodern maritime material culture and technologies.

Recent decades have yielded important shipwreck discoveries around the globe that bear direct witness to the cosmopolitan nature of long-distance trade on the earth's oceans before the modern period. Each section of *Global Ships* highlights illustrative examples from these wrecks that can be used to bring the history of the seas alive for students and fill in important geographic knowledge gaps for non-specialist researchers. Humanities scholars are increasingly interested in the dynamic premodern worlds of the Indian Ocean and other maritime contact zones, but the major material data set from the world's oceans is largely siloed in archaeological literature that many readers outside of the field find inaccessible. A major goal of *Global Ships* is to bridge the gap between the evidence available in recent maritime archaeological work and the research agendas of scholars interested in early globalism and long-distance trade. *Global Ships* scratches the surface of this material through a series of brief sketches of major maritime regions that demonstrate to the non-specialist and student the basic environmental logics and seafaring traditions that have shaped the course of history.

Global Ships is written in the shadow of a largely Eurocentric maritime historiographical tradition that has produced a dramatic narrative of technology that elevates Western sea power while obscuring non-Western shipbuilding traditions. The globalization of European seafaring across the Atlantic and Indian Ocean worlds beginning at the close of the fifteenth century, embodied in the voyages of figures like Christopher Columbus and Vasco da Gama, has long been understood (and taught) as the beginning of a new, modern age, and the end of the isolation and technological backwardness of premodernity (Connery, 2001: 182). These voyages are imagined as the heralds of the *Modern Age*, writ-large, the fulfillment of a teleological promise embedded in the long wait of the European Middle Ages (Armitage, 1992: 51–52). The fifteenth-century ships that accomplished those voyages are painted as the deliverers of that promise and the arks of technological and cultural exceptionalism that made European conquests by sea, somehow, inevitable. But the global history of seafaring makes short shrift of this framing.

The sea presents a problem not only with the ways we measure and divide the boundaries between locations, cultures, and nations, but in the way we measure time. Because we count large scales of human time not in hours and minutes, but in technologies – starting with the Age of stone tools, then bronze and iron metallurgy – our reckoning of when the Modern Age began is similarly shaped by technology. The symbolic dividing line between the premodern past and the Modern present is often conceived as the first sea voyage of Christopher Columbus across the Atlantic Ocean. Like a razor slicing time in two, this transit between the Old and New Worlds ideologically begat a New Global Age with Europe as its protagonist in the Western cultural imagination. If the European Age of Discovery by sea was the genesis of the Modern period, the frame-built ships of European explorers were understood as the Big Bang. In the words of David Armitage, there is "a distinguished pedigree for identifying Atlantic history with 'early' modernity, before the onset of industrialization, mass democracy, the nation state, and all the other classic defining features of full-fledged modernity, a condition whose origins both Adam Smith and Karl Marx associated with the European voyages of discovery and especially with 1492" (Armitage & Braddick, 2002: 12). Smith and Marx were not alone in this identification, Christopher Connery traces this oceanic "activation" of Western history through Hegel, the American rhetoric of manifest destiny, and Alfred Mahan's opus of maritime history, *The Influence of Sea Power upon History* (Connery, 2001: 182–183).

The physical materials of premodern global seafaring technology are compelling evidence that our grand historiographical narratives are foundering. The stakes of a reevaluation of the political and ideological frameworks that shape historiographies of global maritime technology are high. Connery argues that the sea has functioned as the "primary mythic element" of the Western cultural imagination, and the site of the discursive construction of the civilizational self (Connery, 2010: 685–686). Because time is measured with the ideological yardstick of "progress," seafaring technology casts an obscuring, teleological shadow of Eurocentric Modernity, backwards, onto everything that came before. This produces a fundamental erasure of non-Western technologies and people and works discourses of Orientalism and White supremacy[1] into the very foundations of our disciplinary periodizations (Said, 1978; Connery, 2001: 186–189, Connery, 2010: 687). It *others* the past and whitewashes the present and future. In his recent Element in this series, *Swahili Worlds in Globalism*, Chapurukha M. Kusimba argues that understanding cosmopolitan medieval maritime cultures like the Swahili, "requires unscrambling half a millennium of colonization" (Kusimba, 2024: 2).

In Eurocentric periodizations of time, recorded history is divided into the eras of Beginning, Between, and After: Classical Antiquity, the Middle Ages, and the Modern. In this system, the premodern is a moniker of anticipation and absence, defined by its lack of the modern rather than by its own characteristics. The tripartite division of history is a frame story for the rise and fall of Rome and the rise of a new European imperialism by sea (Heng, 2021: 35). In this rubric, the Middle Ages are what fell between two bookend eras of unprecedented European imperial power. For historians of the premodern world beyond European borders, this framework for understanding the past is problematic not just because of its irrelevance when attempts are made to apply it globally, but because many valorized, defining aspects of the "Modern" appear outside of Europe centuries before Europe's "Modernity" had begun (Abu-Lughod, 1989). But what do we do with the evidence of progress and technology dating from Before the Big Bang left in the wake of Columbus's ships? What do we do if the modern is just the premodern, but on another shore?

The "Global Middle Ages" is, itself, a term with a past and a future that requires examination. As other authors in this series have argued, the "Global Middle Ages" label is a tool meant to revise problematic European periodizations which have, for too long, been taken to be axiomatic. It is a chronological net woven to capture a larger set of data than the Eurocentric narrative of the medieval, and though its dating overlaps with Europe's Middle Ages, its inclusion criteria embrace, and face, the world. Scholars of the European Middle Ages who are mindful of the presence and influence of diverse, non-European cultures and people within Europe between the fall of Rome and the rise of the colonial era have used the banner of a more Global Middle Ages to understand the flows of connectivity within Europe in this period (Heng, 2021: 27). Other premodernists whose areas of specialization lay far outside of Europe's borders have also experimented with the term to highlight transregional relationships, to shift scholarly focus away from events

---

[1] Philosopher Charles W. Mills defines White supremacy as a "political system, a particular power structure of formal or informal rule, socioeconomic privilege, and norms for the differential distribution of material wealth and opportunities, benefits and burdens, rights and duties," as "the unnamed political system that has made the modern world what it is today" (Mills, 2014: 1–2).

in Europe and towards the dynamic connectivities and globalism of the Silk Road and Indian Ocean worlds, and to better account for the realities of economic and cultural exchange in Afro-Eurasia between 500 and 1500 CE.

Geraldine Heng has written in her introduction to this series that the act of exporting the framework of "the Middle Ages" beyond Europe's borders can be problematic as a potentially "colonizing gesture" by Euromedievalists who are transporting constructs from their own field to the rest of the world (Heng, 2021: 35). Although the label is fraught and laden with a Eurocentric accounting of temporality, its spatial and ideological decentering of Europe has been useful to scholars and educators who are engaged in critiquing the hegemony of Europe in disciplinary constructs of the past.[2] In outlining the opportunities and constraints of the "Global Middle Ages" label and other descriptive and analytical models of early globalism taken up by scholars, Heng makes clear the very real dangers of eliding the diverse temporalities and accounts of time operative in the distant past (Heng, 2021). Though the spatial framing of historical cores-and-peripheries derived from earlier approaches has a troubling lineage and major analytical lacunae, the framework of the Global Middle Ages provides a methodological opportunity to examine medieval Europe as a periphery to other cosmopolitan cores. This framework comes with its own hazards, as Heng points out, "the very idea that there are "core" centers and "peripheral" outer zones is an idea that many would find objectionable, even offensive" (Heng, 2021: 79). But analytically de-centering Europe from an analysis of world history provides an opportunity to correct for the gravitational pull of colonial, White supremacist mythology masquerading as history.

Periodization is always a narrative device that selects its protagonists and valorizes their historical activities within an otherwise neutral flow of time, and in the tradition of European historiography, it has constructed a narrative Western self in opposition to an Other. Edward Said's analysis of the constructed binary at the heart of Orientalist discourse – *civilization versus barbarity*, *West versus East* – is also applicable to discourses of temporality (Said, 1978). *Present versus past* and *Modern versus Premodern* are constructs laden with "civilizational" bias. The first chapter of the tripartite historiography of Eurocentrism began as an origin story rooted in the Aegean periphery's struggle to grapple with the power of the Persian empire and is rhetorically fused with the genesis of Orientalism, itself. As the Greek tradition came to define itself in opposition to an Eastern Other and subsequent empires appropriated versions of this story for themselves, Classical Antiquity, the Middle Ages, and the Modern were coined as subgenres of a narrative about competing power. The idea of

---

[2] Curtis, P. (2021). "De-Centering the Global Middle Ages." https://prcurtis.com/events/GMA/.

a *medieval* is a dramaturgical one, it is an Act II for the narrative of European exceptionalism, a middle moment between classical Greece and European mastery of the world's seas. The theatricality of this structure conceals, rather than reveals, historical complexity and, most often, historical reality.

If "Modernity" and its signs and symptoms are the goalpost of history, the story began earlier and it began elsewhere. Acknowledging historical periodizations as the framing and narrative arcs of storytelling allows us to monitor what they *do*, and how they select for and delimit their protagonists. If we borrow Charlotte Furth's phrasing about the process of social construction as it relates to the body and apply it to periodization, we can understand time and space as "prisoners of discourse" (Furth, 1999: 25). When we tell stories *about* time and space, and tell stories with them, we are making meaning and making choices. We are selecting our protagonists, and in the case of traditional maritime historiography, those protagonists have sailed for European empires. The label of the "Global Middle Ages" provides an opportunity to interrogate those meanings, to interrogate those choices, and to frame new stories about protagonists that have hitherto been hidden by our methods.

This edition of the Cambridge *Elements in the Global Middle Ages* series seeks to complicate Eurocentric histories of the sea by examining the multifaceted, diverse, and global traditions of seafaring and boatbuilding that preceded the European Age of Exploration. In a nutshell, it asks the questions: what came before the colonial-origin-story of European mastery of the world's oceans, and, in what ways was the early modern globalization of seafaring continuous with and indebted to a global past? By examining boatbuilding traditions of major maritime regions that knit together the global seas between 500 and 1500 CE, *Global Ships* highlights the continuities with the past represented by later ocean navigators, and points past them to paint a portrait of premodern maritime history in a truly global framework. The case studies selected for this text demonstrate the diverse and hybrid origins of the ships of the voyages of exploration and complicate the story of European mastery of the seas.

European navigators who sailed the seas in the so-called Age of Discovery were not the first to do so, and their ships, which have come to carry enormous symbolic meaning in politico-technological discourse, were built and navigated using technologies and innovations from the past. Because the political and ideological stakes are so high in unpacking the maritime history that preceded the Voyages of Discovery, a goal of this study is to provide students and historians who do not focus on maritime materials in their own scholarship with the basic tools to understand the diverse global seafaring technologies that preceded and informed the European Age of Exploration.

This contribution to the *Elements in the Global Middle Ages* series utilizes shipwrecks from around the world as a primary form of historical evidence about the past. Analytically, methodologically, and pedagogically, why do shipwrecks matter for the Global Middle Ages? They are a submerged archive of a world that has largely been erased at the intersections of colonialism, racism, and the technological chauvinism of European Modernity. Shipwrecks are time capsules that, while underwater (and because of the enormous difficulty of their excavation), have avoided disfiguring aspects of the colonial gaze suffered by artifacts recovered and looted on land that have been ripped from temple walls and cut away from their origins. The archaeological recovery of shipwreck materials in the present and in recent decades represents a global crisis of epistemology, politics, and methods and an opportunity to recover the past differently. Natali Pearson argues for a critical cultural heritage approach that would strengthen the "protection and preservation" of shipwrecks by telling their complex stories (Pearson, 2023: 3–5, 16). For the purposes of this study, premodern ships that sailed the world's seas represent a tangible touchstone against which ideological discourse about modernity and seafaring can be reassessed. To unpack the ideology surrounding the capacities and design of the European ships that crossed the Atlantic and the Indian Oceans in the late-fifteenth century, we have to survey what came before. Rather than representing radically new seafaring technology, the ships of Columbus and Vasco da Gama embodied the *longue durée* of globalized technological exchange between maritime regions.

During the Global Middle Ages, maritime trade networks spanning the seas globalized commodities, religions, and trade diasporas in an increasingly mobile world. Focusing on shipbuilding traditions, nautical cultures, sailing itineraries, and examples of recovered shipwrecks and cargoes, *Global Ships* provides an expert overview of the major vessels that sailed the seas in this period. A concise interpretive guide to global maritime technologies and cultures for researchers, teachers, and students, this edition of the Cambridge *Elements in the Global Middle Ages* highlights essential historical context, technological case studies, and logics of seafaring around the world before the modern age. For those interested in diving deeper, each regional sketch can serve as a jumping off point to engage with targeted archaeological literature more directly.

1 A Prehistory of Boatbuilding and Long-Distance Trade Networks

The first section of Global Ships *is a short introduction to the global history of boatbuilding and seafaring in the premodern world, including the development of reed and skin boats, dugout canoes, and wooden-planked vessels and their increasing importance to transregional trade. Key examples of recovered Bronze Age vessels provide a sketch of the important role of transregional maritime trade before Antiquity, and a foundation for understanding the developments in maritime trade to follow.*

The land-based histories we learn, and teach, in school present the political illusion of a world divided into distinct and separate segments, with their boundaries marked out on maps with solid lines. Our academic disciplines are divided into similar area specializations that reproduce these lines of demarcation. But for the majority of human history, people have moved across and between boundaries. The World Ocean is the singular, interconnected, body of water that makes up the majority of the surface of the planet, connecting and surrounding every land mass that dots the Earth's exterior (see Figure 1). When we emerged from the Stone Age, our species had already crossed land and water to populate the globe, and even when we settled into cities and pledged allegiance to particular plots of cultivated land, many continued to move between them with the seasonal rhythms of nomadic pastoralism. Large-scale, long-distance trade on the seas dates from our very earliest experiences of settlement and civilization.

To understand premodern seafaring, it is important to simultaneously hold in your mind's eye the singularity of the World Ocean, with the endless opportunities for connection that it provides, and the plurality of the world's *oceans* as distinct maritime regions. Maritime regions are shaped by the constraints and openings offered by the environment and recent historical approaches to ocean basins and other waterways are rooted in Fernand Braudel's analysis of the Mediterranean (Braudel, 1995; Bentley, 1999). Although the sea as an analytic

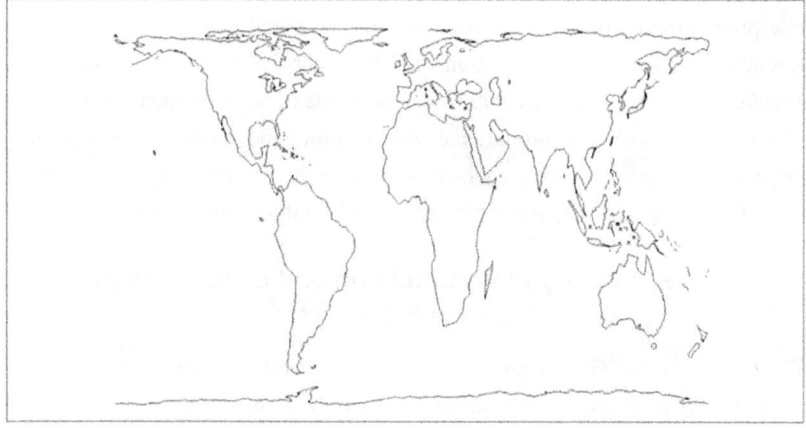

Figure 1 Map illustrating maritime regions described in *Global Ships*

can offer an important corrective to terracentric and Eurocentric political historiography, it is important to understand that the world's maritime regions do come with their own structuring realities. The seas are not a blank slate that mariners can act upon as they might choose, their histories are structured by natural forces every bit as coercive and determining as political power or violence. The structuring powers of wind direction and water currents delimit zones of contact and human activity and shape the seasons of human life. The sections of *Global Ships* that follow trace the relationship between historical human activity and the ecology of major maritime regions in the so-called "Old World" associated with Afro-Eurasia. These very short sketches are intended to equip students and researchers with basic familiarity with the global patchwork of premodern seafaring regions and cultures and introduce them to key contributions to the technology of shipbuilding rooted in each environment.

Because long-distance seafaring has become something of a synonym for modernity in the post-Columbus popular imagination, it is important to begin our discussion of the Global Middle Ages with a snapshot of the prehistory of human mobility on the water. The undivided fluidity of the World Ocean has long served as an engine of human movement and activity, dispersing us across coastal littorals and open sea. Since the Bronze Age, human beings have harnessed the circulations and rhythms of the World Ocean to travel and trade across long, nautical distances – establishing trade routes that still shape circulations of people and materials, to this day. But the primary structuring forces of human activity, historically, on this global body of water are not political lines, borders, or conflicts, but, rather, wind direction and water currents. Gales, monsoons, and trade winds have defined the lines on maritime maps, drawing out routes and durable paths of movement that are not lines of division, but of connection. Their physical and practical genesis is rooted in factors that feel far-removed from political considerations: water temperature, visibility, fog, and the natural architecture of coastlines. These environmental constraints have shaped when and how mariners risk going to sea and have structured the *longue durée* of the seasons and paths of opportunity across the planet (Braudel, 1973).

The majority of the oldest watercraft made by human beings that survive in the archaeological record date from the Neolithic period, when newly organized approaches to food production enabled craftsmen to increasingly devote time and labor to specialized work beyond the needs of daily survival. But the oldest vessel so far recovered is even older, dating from the transitional period between the Paleolithic era and Neolithic revolution, when increasingly sophisticated tools and methods were employed in hunting and gathering.[3] In the Bronze Age,

---

[3] The Mesolithic Pesse canoe of the Netherlands.

long-distance seafaring had begun in earnest. The newly developed technology of metallurgy that defined the Bronze Age required long-distance trade, either by land or sea, to supply the necessary copper and tin that were needed to create bronze alloy objects. These metal routes built upon earlier trade networks that emerged as populations began to rise within settlements after the development of agriculture. As population density increased, cities could no longer produce all of the food necessary to feed their inhabitants and had to rely on trade with outlying areas and larger, more distant regions (Jennings, 2010).

There are four basic approaches to early global boatbuilding that are useful in understanding the seemingly limitless varieties of watercraft that developed around the premodern world (Greenhill, 1995). Very early watercraft included rafts, boats made from animal skin, boats made from bark, and hollowed-out log boats. These approaches would give rise to vessels that were uniquely suited to the specific environmental, commercial, and military contexts of the diverse maritime regions where they operated. The major seafaring traditions that dominated the Global Middle Ages emerged from these methods, utilizing boatbuilding strategies that began by constructing the outward "skin" or "shell" of the boat first, or by beginning with the construction of a frame (McGrail, 2001: 8).

By far the most famous seafaring boats to be excavated from the Bronze Age have been recovered in the waters of the Mediterranean just south of Turkey. The Ulu Burun wreck was a large, wooden-planked vessel dated through dendrochronology to just after 1305 BCE that carried a massive, diverse cargo (see Figure 2) (Pulak, 1998: 214). The ship was loaded with objects not only from across the Mediterranean, but from trade regions well beyond it. The trajectory and cargo of the vessel support an interpretation that the ship was engaged in the east-west transportation of copper from the coast of the Levant, westward, for bronze production (Bass, 1986: 271). At the time of its descent to the seafloor, the Ulu Burun vessel was hauling ten tons of copper ingots, in addition to one ton of tin, and significant quantities of wood, round ingots of colored glass, unworked ivory, orpiment, ceramics, resin, figs, olives, pine nuts, safflower, black cumin, sumac, coriander, whole pomegranates, and other luxury goods like jewelry and thousands of beads including Baltic amber (Pulak, 1998: 206, 210). The artifacts recovered from the wreck also included a hieroglyphic-inscribed ring and scarab, drinking cups, tortoise and ostrich shells, cosmetics containers, an ivory trumpet, weights, and twenty-four anchor stones (Pulak, 1998: 216). Some of these objects may have been intended for official gift exchange, illustrating the role exchange networks have long played not just in the distribution of metals and materials of practical or technological necessity, but in the promotion of social cohesion and alliance-building (Pulak, 1998: 214–215).

Global Ships 11

Figure 2 Display of Ulu Burun Cargo, Bodrum. Modified from the original by sarah_c_murray (www.flickr.com/photos/sarah_c_murray/), used under CC BY-SA 2.0 (https://creativecommons.org/licenses/by-sa/2.0/)

The Ulu Burun vessel provides us with an important case study of the types of information about the past that can be gleaned from a shipwreck and the many methods used by researchers to better understand the world these ships inhabited. For many readers, the early date of the findings associated with the Ulu Burun wreck mark one of the first shocks delivered by the remains of premodern ships. The cargo, which originated in multiple, far-flung locations, documents already complex, long-distance trade relationships in the second millennium BCE and is a time capsule of the objects that were moving across Afro-Eurasia at the dawn of global maritime long-distance trade. The physical structures of boats and cartographic structures of enduring trade routes that would eventually come to define the Global Middle Ages and Modernity have their roots in this cosmopolitan prehistory. It is not only the trade goods onboard the Ulu Burun vessel that tell a story about premodern connection on the seas, but the scraps of wood also left behind from the broken structure of the ship are a snapshot of a moment of technological development and exchange that is characteristic of how boatbuilding technologies would move and adapt across trade routes over time.

The diverse methods used around the world at different points in time to connect the pieces of wood together that comprise the structure of a boat stand out like unique fingerprints in shipwreck vessels and recovering even small pieces of a ship's structure can bring into sharp focus the entire puzzle of its itinerary. Wooden-planked boats reveal technological traditions, genealogies, and exchanges between maritime regions that provide strong clues for the origins of a ship when evaluated alongside other evidence. Sewn boats from the premodern western Indian Ocean region are distinguishable from lashed-lug vessels from Southeast Asia, and the presence of dowels, nails, fastenings, joints, or other structural features that point towards frame-first versus hull-first construction methods are all readily visible in shipwreck remains. The ever-present obstacle to identification is the speed with which organic remains like wood and cord degrade and, ultimately, disappear underwater in most marine environments.

Sometimes small pieces of a ship's structure survive by being buried and covered over in the wrecking process. Several telling pieces of the Ulu Burun ship survived and have been recovered by archaeologists. In addition to fragments of oars that were found at the site, a portion of the rudimentary keel-plank of the ship made of fir wood, which would have served as a kind of longitudinal spine for the body of the boat, was recovered alongside cedar planks fastened by peg-locked, oak mortise-and-tenon joints (Bass, 1986: 269, 275).

From the outside, mortise-and-tenon joints appear to connect adjoining planks of wood seamlessly, but in fact, conceal the coupling of two intersecting pieces of wood that fit together via a protruding tab on one end with a depression on the other (see Figure 3). They also conceal a techno-civilizational rivalry about where they were invented, and refined, and who can take credit for the role they played in the history of seafaring. The presence of this type of locked joint in the wreckage is very significant, it is the oldest example of locked mortise-and-tenon, shell-first construction in an actual seafaring vessel that has so far been discovered and this technology would continue to be in use in the Mediterranean well into the Global Middle Ages (Pulak, 1998: 210). Researchers have theorized

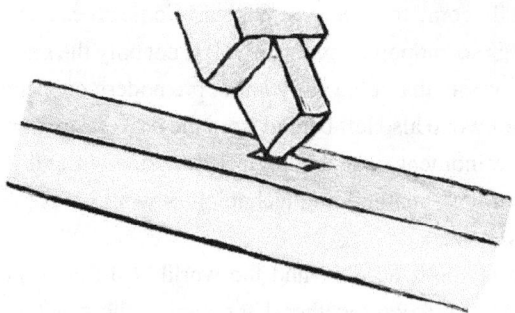

Figure 3 A mortise-and-tenon joint

that mortise-and-tenon joints were transferred technology from Egypt to the Levant, but Egyptian examples of mortise-and-tenon joints were fastened together through sewing, rather than by locking them with extra wooden pegs, like we see in the Ulu Burun wreckage. It has been speculated that the locked mortise-and-tenon joints recovered in Bronze Age shipwrecks like the Ulu Burun might reflect an early Canaanite, Proto-Phoenician innovation to this Egyptian technology by adding locking pegs to joints under the ship's waterline (McGrail, 2001: 125, 133–134). Other objects on the vessel like the anchor stones, writing boards, drinking vessels, and assorted personal belongings and tools used by the crew confirm the likelihood of an origin for the ship in the eastern Mediterranean, including the jawbone of a house mouse that most closely resembles species from Syria (McGrail, 2001: 124; Cucchi, 2008: 2953). Although science can tell us the origins of objects from the wreck, structural details like the mortise-and-tenon joints demonstrate that the more interesting question may be what shipwreck remains, themselves, can tell us about the global history of science and technology.

Egyptian boatbuilding in the Bronze Age united the know-how of river travel along the Nile with the structural wherewithal of voyaging along the coasts of the Mediterranean and the Red Sea. Earlier Bronze Age boats like the famous Egyptian Khufu solar barge have been recovered from funerary contexts on land and their wooden joints are primarily sewn and lashed. Stripped bitumen waterproofing fragments dated from the third millennium BCE that were recovered from the coast of Oman were encrusted with the markings of barnacles and have preserved what appear to be impressions left from binding material on reed bundles, matting, or wooden planks (Vosmer, 2000: 235). The approach of binding reed bundles into early river rafts and bitumen-coated boats that was practiced in the Nile and Tigris-Euphrates River valleys may have influenced not only the forms of early flat-bottomed Egyptian wooden-planked boats, but the technique of lashing wooden planks together in later forms of shipbuilding across the western Indian Ocean region (Greenhill & Morrison, 1995: 86; McGrail, 2001: 23).

Exchange is built into the very bodies of the earliest seafaring boats from the Bronze Age: Egyptian wooden-planked boats required imported timber from the Levant and bitumen from Mesopotamia (McGrail, 2001: 16). In the same way that the sea has defied boundaries, so has technology- boats and ships are always artifacts of connection and indices of exchange. Boatbuilding technology is interstitial. Where a shipwreck is located underwater may be far afield from its point of origin, and the chain of technological exchanges that contributed to its materials, design, and construction reflect a deeply interconnected world.

Although the size and cargo of the Ulu Burun ship suggest the activities and interests of Bronze Age elites, seafaring has always included every stratum of society. The artifacts recovered from another Bronze Age Canaanite-Syrian ship near the Ulu Burun, dating from approximately 1200 BCE, demonstrate the vitality of early seafaring through the lens of a very different cargo (Bass et al., 1967: 41–42, 84, 116; McGrail, 2001: 124). The Cape Gelidonya wreck contained copper, tin, and bronze ingots, but it had a significant assemblage of metal tools, metal-casting waste, weights, anvils, and collected scrap metal onboard (Bass et al., 1967: 163). The scrap metal, in the form of broken objects, and the casting waste and metalworking equipment onboard suggest that this vessel was engaged in cabotage, moving from port to port, while collecting, repairing, and creating bronze objects (Bass et al., 1967: 121). The wreckage also contained personal property, supplies, and materials for the use of the crew: a worn cylinder seal, fish bones, olive pits, small pieces of baskets and mats, five scarabs potentially used as amulets or souvenirs, and a single animal knucklebone used for a game (like dice) or for divination (Bass et al., 1967: 133–134, 144, 148, 160). All of these materials, taken together, paint the portrait of an itinerant metalworker and merchant moving through the Bronze Age Mediterranean (Bass et al., 1967: 163). Though far less grand than the Ulu Burun vessel and its luxurious cargo, the Cape Gelidonya vessel also had locked, mortise-and-tenon planking.

The cylinder seal onboard the Cape Gelidonya vessel illustrates one of the most important contributions of Bronze Age long-distance trade to global culture: writing. The writing systems of Egypt, Mesopotamia, and the Indus River valley developed in close proximity to each other and were used for accounting and business. Writing, itself, was a technology made necessary by the robust movement of people and goods in the period. The later Phoenician descendants of the Canaanite seafarers who piloted the Cape Gelidonya and Ulu Burun ships spread their alphabet, which was born from the cultural exchange between Egypt and the Levant, across the Mediterranean after the Bronze Age collapse, giving rise to a global family of alphabetic writing systems still in use today. Cultural practices, communication, ideas, and beliefs have always spread by ship alongside cargoes full of metals, grains, and luxury items since the beginning of long-distance seafaring.

One object recovered from the Ulu Burun wreck is a particularly poignant reminder of the invention of writing and the precarious position of the maritime past in modern historiography. The Ulu Burun vessel wrecked while carrying a Near Eastern writing set comprised of two wooden writing boards that closed into a position resembling a codex. The interior of the boards would have been covered in beeswax at the time the ship sailed the Mediterranean, and the wax would have been written on with a stylus (Payton, 1991). The wax and the words that sank with the ship are long gone, but the excavation of the writing set from the seafloor calls up the image of the missing histories of the sea that have not made it into our archives or narratives about the past. Why has the premodern maritime past inhabited such a slippery position in historical discourse? Maritime historiography is precariously positioned on fault lines that define and divide our political narratives of both place and period. Human activity on the sea straddles the line between prehistory and written records yet shapes our grandest narratives of conquest and progress. Global maritime historiography is riddled with highly political and ideological erasures that efface the contributions of premodern, non-Western seafarers.

2 Austronesian Boatbuilding and Seafaring, Southeast Asian Lashed-Lug Vessels

The second section of Global Ships *focuses on the boat and shipbuilding technologies of premodern Austronesian seafarers, including outrigger and double-hulled boats that enabled the earliest long-distance oceanic voyages across Maritime Southeast Asia and the Pacific. The increasing importance and oceanic reach of Southeast Asian lashed-lug vessels to regional and transregional trade networks is also explored through case studies of lashed-lug shipwrecks recovered from the tenth through the thirteenth centuries.*

Millennia before the voyages of Christopher Columbus or Vasco da Gama, the beginning of an entirely different colonization by sea was unfolding in Asian waters. Historical linguists, geneticists, and archaeologists have studied a trail of artifacts, languages, and DNA left in its wake across the waters of the Pacific and Indian Oceans. Though scholarly understandings of the motivations and social mechanisms that drove what is now known as the Austronesian expansion are contentious, the lasting geographic range of this large-scale cultural movement by sea is unparalleled.

The Austronesian expansion unfolded across the waters of Southeast Asia and Oceania beginning between five- and six-thousand years ago. Seafarers, likely initially voyaging from the southern coast of China, began to spread and settle outward, first reaching Taiwan and then, by 4500 years ago, the Philippines (Jiao et al., 2002; Bellwood, 2004; Bellwood & Dizon, 2005; Anderson & O'Connor, 2008: 4). The dispersal of stone adzes across the Taiwan Strait in the Neolithic period, the gradual spread of pottery and agricultural products over centuries and nautical miles, and genetic and historical linguistic connections spanning the region have fueled generations of research. The expansion of Austronesian seafarers from the South China Sea outward, into the Pacific, led to the population of Outer Oceania by 1000 BCE (Rolett et al., 2000; Tsang, 2002; Anderson & O'Connor, 2008; Terrell, 2009; Lansing et al., 2011). Another Element in this series, *Oceania: 800-1800 CE*, by James L. Flexner, explores the "burst of voyaging and discovery" that radiated outward across Polynesia from 900-1100 CE (Kirch, 2017; Flexner, 2021: 12). As a result of each of these waves of migration, Austronesian languages and cultural practices diffused on a massive scale, to over half of the planet. In the words of archaeologist, John Miksic, "no other language family matched this feat until the British established their empire in the eighteenth century" (Miksic, 2013: 26).

The frequent use of the explanatory model of colonization to describe the expansive Austronesian settlements spanning such a vast region over many centuries may not be appropriate, and may reflect modern paradigms of sea expansion and power. But the waves of migration continued, impacting seafaring practices around the world. Between 500 and 1000 CE, seafarers from Austronesia crossed the Indian Ocean and settled in Madagascar, making their geographic reach, which now spanned all the way from the Pacific to the eastern coast of Africa, a testament to human ingenuity and a defining feature of the Global Middle Ages (Jiao, 2021; Serva and Pasquini, 2022).

Although the earliest forms of watercraft used in the Austronesian expansion do not survive in the archaeological record, key technological contributions to global seafaring can be traced to this, and subsequent, waves of their migration. The outrigger boat, which adds a supporting external flotation structure to the main hull of a watercraft, provided the stability to successfully navigate the unique maritime region of Oceania (see Figure 4). Older, flat-bottomed sea rafts

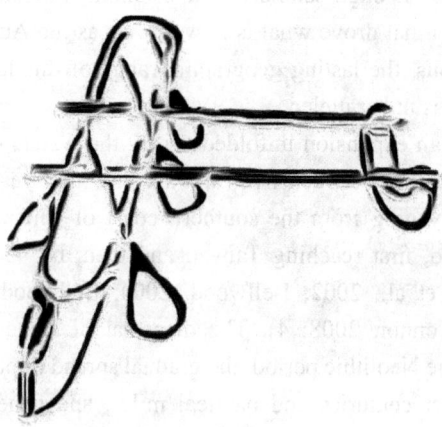

Figure 4 An outrigger boat

were enhanced with the addition of hollowed-out logs which were gradually adapted into attached canoes, double-hulled vessels, and auxiliary flotation structures. Outriggers were attached to a vessel by booms and ribbing that was secured to the interior of the hull through lashing, providing increased stability (Horridge, 2008: 89).

The combination of the use of stabilized outriggers with the invention of the crab-claw, triangular sail enabled Austronesian seafarers to tack against the prevailing winds of the Pacific more safely, exploring outlying islands that they could see on the horizon, while safely riding the dominant winds back home (see Figure 5) (Horridge, 2004: 143). This combination of innovations demonstrates a reality we see across global maritime regions, that boat-building technologies develop in response to the specific environmental conditions in which they emerge. Available materials are put to use to address the specific contexts of wind direction, current, water depth, and purpose that are unique from place to place. As boat-building traditions emerge and come into contact with each other through long-distance trade, methods merge and hybrid traditions begin to encompass larger regions. In the case of the innovation of the advantageous pairing of outrigger, external flotation with triangular, crab-claw sails, a technological tool kit that could tack against the wind set the stage for an extended Austronesian Age of Exploration. These technologies would continue to be critical for long-distance trade vessels in multiple maritime regions during the Global Middle Ages.

Recognizing the unique environmental origins of global boat-building traditions not only reveals the historical local logics of seafaring but puts the lie to the technological chauvinism in colonial discourse, which still heavily pervades

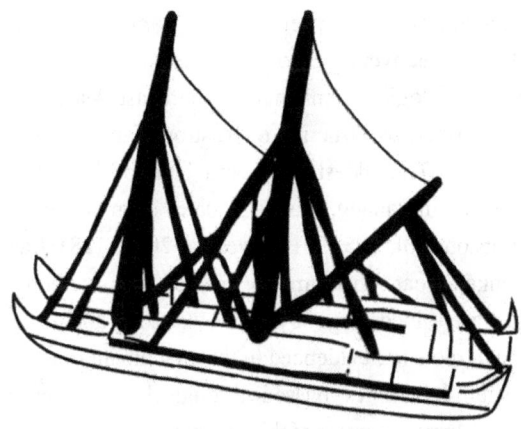

Figure 5 Crab-claw sails

Eurocentric maritime historiography and public perception. Because of its role in the so-called European Age of Exploration, the triangular sail is possibly the most contentious object in global maritime material culture, with multiple regions claiming responsibility for its invention. Scholars of the Pacific and Southeast Asia have argued for a recognition of Austronesian origins for this technology (Horridge, 2004: 146). Manguin and others argue that although the technologies embodied in early outrigger canoes and the triangular, crab-claw sail certainly travelled with the Austronesian seafarers who navigated from Southeast Asia to Madagascar in the first millennium CE, it is likely that these voyages across the Indian Ocean were made in larger vessels that were well-equipped for the journey (Manguin, 2016: 63). The rigging of these ships provides an opportunity for reflection on transregional developments to rigging that would follow.

The triangular lateen, or Latin, sail enabled the fifteenth-century "voyages of discovery," and its addition to traditional Mediterranean sails gave rise to the full rigging of European sailing ships in the medieval and early modern periods. The triangular, lateen sail has become a lightning rod for claims of European exceptionalism because of its technological edge in navigating against the wind and its critical role in propelling the ships of conquest across the oceans. The fact that it has complicated cultural origins is a fly in the ointment to Eurocentric accounts of boatbuilding, particularly because of the role of Muslim seafarers in spreading its use into the Mediterranean. Earlier characterizations of the lateen sail's introduction from the Indian Ocean world to the Mediterranean via Arabs after the advent of Islam have been revised to account for pre-Islamic seafaring in the Near East and the role of Persian merchants in the pre-Islamic Indian Ocean, in particular (Whitewright, 2009: 98; Respess, 2020a). The lack of surviving examples of lateen sails in the archaeological record from this transition presents challenges to interpreting iconographic representations of sails and remains of masts recovered in contact zones.

The earliest archaeological remnants of Southeast Asian boats preserve the outrigger-derived, lashed construction of Austronesian vessels (Horridge, 2004; Lacsina, 2015: 126). The oldest recovered boat of lashed-lug construction, discovered in Pontian in Pahang, Malaysia, dates from between the third to fifth centuries CE (Gibson-Hill, 1951: 111; Lacsina, 2015: 128). Lashed-lug vessels are wooden-planked boats that employ a shell-first method of construction where the planks are joined, edge-to-edge, by sewing and, quite often, dowels. Their Austronesian roots are evidenced in the attachment of the ribs of the frame to the ship's shell by lashes passed through lugs, which are protrusions on the hull planks. Many examples of this characteristically lashed-lug Southeast-Asian construction have survived from the Global Middle Ages in the form of shipwrecks across the region. The Sumatran, lashed-lug Kolam Pinisi boat dates from between the fifth and seventh centuries CE, and remains from several lashed-lugged boats have been identified in Butuan in the Philippines, dating from the late eighth to early tenth centuries (Lacsina, 2015: 128–129). Numerous other examples have been identified on and near the coasts of Thailand, Vietnam, the Philippines, Brunei, Malaysia, and Indonesia (Kimura, 2016).

By the third century BCE, Southeast Asian seafarers had arrived at the Bay of Bengal, and a bustling trade of Moluccan spices for bronze circulated throughout the region (Miksic, 2013: 26). By the first century BCE spices from Molucca had already made their way to the Han Dynasty capital at Chang'an, the eastern terminus of the Silk Road (Miksic, 2013: 26). Over the centuries that followed, Southeast Asian spices would become increasingly important luxury items as far away as the Roman empire. From the first–sixth centuries of the Common Era, mainland Southeast Asia, Sumatra, and Java developed progressively expansive sea trade-oriented economies (Manguin, 2016: 55). *Southeast Asian Interconnections*, another Element in this series by Derek Heng, describes the development of premodern shipping networks throughout the region and the expansion of transregional long-distance trade (Heng, 2022).

Southeast Asia was an important cultural and economic core of the Global Middle Ages. Local commodities drew long-distance seafarers from both sides of the Indian Ocean littoral and the South China Sea, and its port cities became not only emporia for local and regional products, but entrepots for transregional exchange. The polities of Funan, Champa, and the Shailendran, Srivijayan, and Majapahit thalassocracies made the larger Southeast Asian maritime region a center of global trade. Ninth-century depictions of ships at the Borobudur temple site in Java (see Figure 6) provide unique visual evidence of vessels navigating in Southeast Asia during this period. Eleven bas relief carvings of boats are visible at the Buddhist site and contain details of structural features like outriggers (Inglis, 2014).

Geoff Wade has argued that the years 900–1300 CE represent an "early age of commerce" in Southeast Asia that prefigured the globalization in the region that would follow (Wade, 2009: 221). The cargoes of two tenth-century shipwrecks from the region illustrate the role played by lashed-lug vessels in this era of dynamic long-distance trade. The Intan and Cirebon wrecks were both recovered in the Java Sea, and both vessels seem to have been voyaging between Sumatra and Java (Flecker, 2002: 30; Liebner, 2014: v; Mathers and Flecker, 1997). The 300-ton cargo of the Cirebon, which was salvaged in 2005, included Chinese ceramics, Near Eastern glass, Arabic-inscribed beads, and other materials from India, East Africa, and multiple regions of Southeast Asia (Liebner, 2014: 19; Needell, 2018: 69). Because of the nature of the salvage

Figure 6 A Borobudur ship

process, very little of the structure of the ship was methodically studied. However, twenty-six strakes, which are the longitudinal planks running from the front to the back of the hull, were recovered. These planks were conjoined and edge-fastened with dowels, and then framing was attached by lashing through the lugs on the interior side of each plank (Liebner, 2014: 243). This construction method is the hallmark of Southeast Asian boatbuilding in the Global Middle Ages.

The Intan wreck, which was excavated from the northwestern Java Sea in 1997, was also loaded with high-quality Chinese ceramics, Chinese coins, elephant tusks, worked ivory, Near Eastern glass beads, bronze, iron, tin, gold, silver, and a large number of candlenuts (Flecker, 2001: 30, 92, 122; Respess, 2020a: 137, 140). Enough fragments of the hull were recovered to determine that the wreck was made using lashed-lug construction, and a surprising group of objects recovered from the wreck shed additional light on the technology of seafaring in this period.

Almost 400 candlenuts (*Aleurites moluccana*) were recovered from the wreckage, and there is a strong possibility that they were used as a fuel source for torches. Candlenut torches have been associated with night sailing across Oceania and the dispersal of candlenuts across the Pacific mirrors the routes of the Austronesian expansion. The use of lighting aboard ships at night is to be expected on long-distance voyages, but candlenut torches provide the additional advantage of measuring time, which is a critical navigational tool. Candlenuts of uniform sizes burn for equal periods, and a speared-torch made of candlenuts of equal size will count off segments of time on a journey (Hough, 1893: 207; Söderström, 1938: 69, 77; Morton, 1992: 253; Flecker, 2001: 30, 92, 122; Respess, 2020a: 109–113).

This has provocative implications for the history of maritime navigation and is one of the many features of Austronesian seafaring that are deserving of further study.

3 Sewn-Boats from the Western Indian Ocean

The third section of Global Ships *examines sewn-boat traditions from the western Indian Ocean, highlighting the methods of construction and sources of materials for dhows built in Eastern Africa, the Hadramawt coast, the Persian Gulf, and India during the Global Middle Ages. As vehicles for profound transregional cultural exchange, the diversity of dhows from the western ocean littoral represents unique adaptations to local environments and the demands of sailing long-distance trade routes dominated by the monsoon. Two examples of sewn ships from the western Indian Ocean that were recovered in Southeast Asia exemplify the interconnections that can be uncovered by a careful analysis of global ships.*

Muslim merchants operating in the Indian Ocean of the Global Middle Ages were at the center of a vast network of land and sea trade routes that connected all of Afro-Eurasia. Building on the maritime traffic of Persian merchants along the ocean littoral in Late Antiquity, early Muslim seafarers spread Islam to Southeast Asia and China and established enclaves in port cities along the coasts. Burgeoning trade routes and merchant settlements across the growing Islamicate Indian Ocean rendered this maritime space into a cross-cultural contact zone that has, in recent times, been described as a "Muslim Lake" or "Islamic Sea" (Chaudhuri, 1985; Alpers, 2014; Gooding, 2020: 193). The ships left behind by these voyages are revealing new lines of evidence for understanding connectivity in the Global Middle Ages.

The tenth-century Muslim seafarer, Abū Zayd al-Sīrāfī, inadvertently left behind not only detailed information about shipbuilding in the western Indian Ocean in his account of travelling to China and India, but a telling snapshot of his sense of place and experience of the trade routes. He recounts the found wreckage of what he describes as Arab ships that were discovered in the Mediterranean Sea, writing that "these ships had broken up and their crews had been lost; the waves had pounded their hulls to pieces" (al-Sīrāfī, 2014: 86–87). Curiously, to our modern-day cartographic perspective, he does not entertain the possibility that these boats could have originated in the Mediterranean. Instead, he views their appearance there as physical evidence that the Indian Ocean and South China Sea – their normal sailing ground – must have been directly connected to the Mediterranean by a northern passage. He envisions an undiscovered, continuous seaway stretching to the north of the Silk Road, and hypothesizes that this must be the conduit of these broken materials. He writes that after the ships were initially destroyed, ostensibly in the familiar terrain of the Indian Ocean or South China Sea, that the wreckage was:

> driven by winds and currents which cast the planks into the Sea of the Khazars [the Caspian Sea]. From there, the timbers floated through the Gulf of al-Rūm [the Azov and Black Seas], finally emerging into the Mediterranean Sea. This points to the fact that the ocean turns north around China and al-Sīlā [Korea], continues around the back of the lands of the Turks and the Khazars, then debouches through the Gulf of al-Rūm, arriving at the Levant. (al-Sīrāfī, 2014: 86–87)

Al-Mas'ūdī, who writes in the same period, largely agrees, asserting about the discovery of the wreckage that "this proves, and God knows best, that the seas are all connected, and that the sea of China and the land of Sila curves around the land of the Turks and ends in the seas of the West through certain inlets of the surrounding Ocean" (al-Mas'ūdī, 2020: 177). They both expand the evidence for this northern seaway to include the circulation of ambergris into the Mediterranean, and al-Mas'ūdī lists the sea attacks by Vikings on Islamic Spain as additional proof of this northern route (al- Mas'ūdī, 2020: 176).

Although modern-day readers will recognize the flaws in this mapping of the world, it points to several defining features of connectivity during this period. First, for both al-Sīrāfī and al-Mas'ūdī, whose cosmopolitan perspectives were deeply rooted in the major ports of the Persian Gulf, certain shipbuilding technologies were so thoroughly associated with Arab seafaring in the Indian Ocean that their appearance, even as orphan planks, had to be understood as artifacts of this tradition. Second, the idea that these ships must have been destined for the eastern Indian Ocean and China was also a given, as was the presumption that their destruction through wreckage, in all likelihood, occurred in eastern waters. These assumptions are significant and signal the biases formed by the norms of sea trade between the Persian Gulf and Indian Ocean in the centuries leading up to these remarks. The ports of the Gulf were the western termini of the oceanic superhighway of long-distance trade between the Islamicate world and China during the Global Middle Ages, and this reality shaped al-Sīrāfī and al-Mas'ūdī's views of the world. Both described the waters of Southeast Asia and China as particularly dangerous, and recent decades of shipwreck finds in the region certainly bear this out. Furthermore, the seasonal monsoon of the Indian Ocean that facilitated journeys across the sea routes, did, in fact, generate winds and warm water currents from Southeast Asia and the South China Sea that came from the south in the summer, pushing sailors northward and allowing them to reach the Chinese coast. The idea of an

Figure 7 Sewn planks

orphaned Arab wreck drifting on these currents, endlessly northbound, into a speculated sea route would be grounded within key experiences of seasoned sailors on the Maritime Silk Road.

Aside from al-Sīrāfī's and al-Mas'ūdī's envisioned map of the world, why were the orphaned planks of wood observed in the Mediterranean understood by these authors to be Arab? What about them, in particular, would invite the assemblage of such a specific back story? Al-Sīrāfī describes the wood from the discovered "Arab" boats as sewn, and says that this method of construction distinguished them as having been made at Siraf, on the Persian coast[4] (see Figure 7). He contrasts their sewn construction against boats made in the Levant or the Eastern Roman world, which he reports were all put together with nails (al-Sīrāfī, 2014: 86). Elsewhere in his travel account he further describes the method used by Omani shipwrights to sew boats for use on the Indian Ocean, detailing their method of twisting rope from coconut fibers to stitch together wooden planks into the hulls of sturdy ships (al-Sīrāfī, 2014: 119–121). Al-Mas'ūdī confirms the identification of the shipwrecked, orphan timbers on the basis of their sewn construction. Writing that the ship planks, which he adds were found near Crete, were drilled teak wood sewn together by coconut fibers, he adds that only boats made for sail in the Indian Ocean used this technique. The unique waters of the Indian Ocean, he writes, destroy iron nails, causing them to disintegrate, a fate that he argues can only be avoided with the deployment of sewn-boat construction[5] (al-Mas'ūdī, 2020: 177). Though later western travelers who were unfamiliar with the advantages of

---

[4] The use of the term Arab for the Persian port of Siraf is al-Sīrāfī's, not mine.
[5] Which he calls the Abyssinian Sea

sewn-boat technology derided it as being inferior to European iron-nail construction, more informed sources like Ibn Battuta argued for the superiority of sewn-boats in the context of the sometimes-rough waters of the Indian Ocean. He praised the resiliency of sewn planks and warned against the dangers of iron-nailed hulls, which he saw as more likely to break apart (Gibb, 1929: 243; Agius, 2005: 36)

It is appropriate that perhaps the two most striking examples of sewn-boat construction from the western Indian Ocean tradition dating from the Global Middle Ages were not recovered on the western side of the littoral, but nearer to their points of destination in the east. The Phanom Surin shipwreck in Thailand, and the Belitung wreck, found in Indonesian waters, likely date to the eighth and ninth centuries CE and bear the clear technological stamp of having been constructed in the western Indian Ocean region.[6] The Belitung wreck is believed to have set sail from the Abbasid Persian Gulf and made the journey to the coast of Tang China, where it was loaded with several tons of luxury goods and ceramics. Most striking in the cargo recovered from the ship were over 56,000 bowls made in the kilns of Changsha, China for the export market (see Figure 8). The ship was wrecked in Southeast Asia on its return voyage to the Middle East, and enough of the structure survived, even after so many centuries spent under water, to identify key elements of its construction (Flecker, 2010: 102–103, 117–118).

Michael Flecker, the archaeologist who oversaw the second phase of the recovery of the ship, describes a visible, surviving (though collapsed) structure on the seafloor with a 15.3-meter keel, a stempost joined to the front of the keel with a mortise-and-tenon joint, a keelson-like apparatus, through-beams that were stitched to the body of the ship, and edge-to-edge, dowel-less sewn planking (Flecker, 2010: 101–103, 117). Samples from the wood recovered from the structure of the ship have been identified as *Afzelia Africana* and *Afzelia bipindensis*, both species from Africa, and teak, which was likely from India (Flecker, 2010: 117). These remains make it abundantly clear that the Belitung vessel was constructed in the western Indian Ocean region, though it is hard to pinpoint exactly where. India, the Persian Gulf, the Arabian peninsula, and eastern Africa all share a history of sewn-boat construction methods, and wood from inland Africa, the Levant, and India had long been exported to regions along the Nile and Mesopotamia that lacked timber appropriate for shipbuilding (Flecker, 2010: 102, 114, 117). The presence of dunnage,

---

[6] A recent article by amateur historian, Mr. Stephen G. Haw, contests the Western Indian Ocean origin of the Belitung ship, but his analysis is based on misrepresentation of the lab analysis of ship timbers and findings of the excavating archaeologist (Haw, S. G., 2019). The scholarly consensus that the ship set sail in the western Indian Ocean remains unchanged.

Figure 8 Belitung Ship Model Sailing a Sea of Changsha Bowls, Asian Civilizations Museum, Singapore

or branches used to support and brace the cargo during packing, from Africa indicates that the ship almost certainly previously docked at a port in East Africa. But there is not enough textual or archaeological evidence to narrow down whether the Belitung ship may have been built in the Persian Gulf region, East Africa, or elsewhere in the western littoral of the Indian Ocean world. The stitching chord and plank wadding recovered from the wreck are likely sea hibiscus fibers and *Melaleuca cajuputi* (Flecker, 2010: 117). Because sewn ships require regular maintenance and re-stitching, these Asian plant remains seem to be evidence of repairs made in Southeast Asia (Flecker, 2010: 118; Respess, 2020a: 59).

The cargo of the Belitung ship is one of the most extraordinary ever recovered and provides an enormous dataset of information about long-distance trade between the western and eastern poles of the Indian Ocean contact zone. The Changsha ceramics onboard bear unique designs and inscriptions and comprise the largest assemblage of late Tang Dynasty ceramics ever found (see Figure 9) (Guy in Krahl et al., 2010: 58). Clearly designed for the export market, these objects are decorated with paintings of natural scenes, animals, calligrams, and Arabic script (Respess, 2020b: 64; Respess, 2020b). The wreck also contained Islamic glass, Persian ceramics, Chinese metalware, and multiple storage jars still packed with intact spices (see Figures 10 and 11) (Flecker and Guy in Krahl et al., 2010).

Figure 9 Belitung Ship Changsha Ceramics Storage, Asian Civilizations Museum, Singapore

Figure 10 Storage Jar from the Belitung Ship, Asian Civilizations Museum, Singapore

Eight miles from the Gulf of Thailand, in the Chao Phraya-Tha chin delta, the Phanom Surin shipwreck was discovered in saturated, reclaimed land (Guy, 2017: 179–180; Komoot, 2021b). Excavations began in 2014 and wooden planking with drilled sewing holes and rope were recovered from the muddy site (Guy, 2017: 180). The structure of the ship is very similar to the Belitung vessel, though larger, and the cargo also clearly demonstrates a connection to the western Indian Ocean routes (Connan et al., 2020). In addition to Chinese ceramics, a turquoise-glazed Persian jar and multiple torpedo jars (so named for their shape) from the Persian Gulf were recovered from the wreck site (Guy, 2017: 185). The torpedo jars were lined with waterproofing bitumen originating in the Persian Gulf, and one jar was inscribed with a Middle Persian, late

Global Ships 27

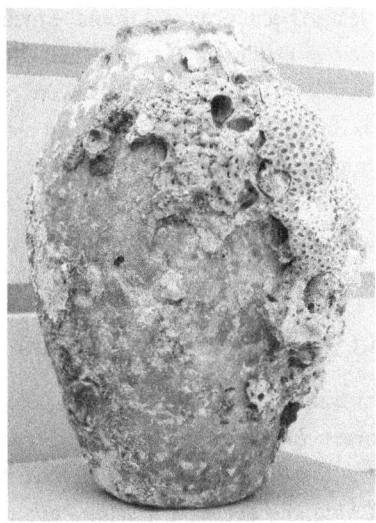

Figure 11 Storage Jar from the Belitung Ship, Asian Civilizations Museum, Singapore

Pahlavi inscription (Connan et al., 2020: 105). Pahlavi inscriptions have also been found in China, India, and Sumatra (Guy, 2017: 188). The Phanom Surin inscription is somewhat ambiguous and has been variously rendered as, "*Yazd-bōzēd*," or the measurement "40" followed by a label for liquid bitumen (Skjærvø in Guy, 2017: 188; Choksy & Nematollahi, 2018: 147). *Yazd-bōzēd* is a proper name which means "God delivers" and John Guy argues that this inscription, and the other Pahlavi inscriptions across the region, reflect a significant role played by Persian traders in the Indian Ocean before the ninth century when Arabic replaced Middle Persian as the dominant written language (Guy, 2017: 188, 191). It is worth noting that *Yazd-bōzēd* is a name associated with the Nestorian community in this period.

The sewn boats of the western Indian Ocean tradition have complex and diverse origins that are obscured by the near-universal application of the term dhow to these vessels in European discourse. Wooden-planked, sewn boats with lateen sails have been known in European sources as dhows from at least the eighteenth century (Agius, 2005: 13). Although the Belitung and Phanom Surin ships are, at present, the only shipwrecks from this tradition dating from the Global Middle Ages to have been recovered from archaeological sites, a few examples of ship timbers have been discovered in Egypt and Oman. Thirty-six hull planks and fourteen other wooden ship remains have been recovered from the coastal site of al-Balīd in Oman. The timbers were bitumen-treated with remnants of the stitching remaining (Belfioretti & Vosmer, 2010; Ghidoni, 2021: 225).

Sewn-boat timbers have also been recovered from the medieval necropolis in the Red Sea port of Quseir al-Qadim in Egypt (Blue, 2002: 149; Blue, 2006; Blue et al., 2011). In both cases, the sewn planks were recycled from ships for use in building projects on land- lintels, shelving, and ceilings in the case of al-Balīd and grave construction in Quseir al-Qadim (Blue, 2002; Ghidoni, 2021). The possibility of new finds across the expansive Indian Ocean world holds open the door to more archaeological data that might clarify questions of specific, local technologies and techniques.

4 Hybrid Ships in China and Southeast Asia

Section four of Global Ships *delves into the hybrid ships that emerged from maritime contact between East Asian shipbuilding traditions and Southeast Asian technologies. The development of flat-bottomed boats for trade on the rivers and canals of China and deeper seafaring hulls on the East China Sea gave way to hybrid seafaring ship designs on the southern coast that reflected China's increasingly direct maritime engagement with Southeast Asia.*

The unique terrain of coastal China's distinct maritime regions gave rise to the emergence of different shipbuilding traditions along China's littoral in premodern history. Maritime archaeologist, Jun Kimura, has outlined distinctive approaches to the construction of watercraft in the premodern Yellow Sea and East China Sea in his book, *The Archaeology of East Asian Shipbuilding* (Kimura, 2016: 15–17). The Yellow Sea region, along the northern coast of the country, was home to flat-bottomed ships designed for easy passage through inland waterways and the shallow waters of the coast (Kimura, 2016: 15). Chinese-constructed vessels in this contact zone with Korea and Japan featured transverse structural supports in the form of bulkheads, which divided the hull into partitioned segments. The presence of bulkheads in Chinese vessels was a defining characteristic of ships constructed up and down the coast during the Global Middle Ages, and is regarded as an important technological development in the history of seafaring. Korean vessels in the Yellow Sea during this period did not possess bulkheads, but rather utilized strong, transverse beams for structural support (Kimura, 2016: 15).

The use of watertight bulkheads in shipbuilding emerged in China around the fifth century CE and was in widespread use by the Tang Dynasty, as evidenced by the remains of surviving river boats from this period (Cai et al., 2010: 26; Kimura, 2016: 6–8). China's relationship to the global trade routes developed dramatically during the Global Middle Ages, with territorial expansion in the northwest putting the Chinese capital cities of Chang'an and Luoyang in direct contact with the Silk Road land routes while colonial expansion to the south enabled increased trade by sea. The Sui and subsequent Tang Dynasties built a system of canals connecting the East China Sea to the major rivers, and these rivers to the capitals to supply the growing urban population with food and supplies (Lewis, 2012). The trade relationship between the Persian Gulf and China exploded after the Abbasid Revolution and the development of the city of Baghdad in the eighth century, and Chinese ports increasingly became host to foreign ships and foreign merchants.

Shipbuilding increased in the Song and Yuan periods, and political changes made the southern maritime economy an imperial priority (Lo, 1955: 489; Heng, 2008; Kimura, 2016: 17, 178; Heng, 2019). Whereas ships constructed in northern China consisted of wooden-planked, flat-bottomed boats that were best suited for travel in rivers, canals, and in the unique shallow coastal waters of the Yellow Sea, the shipbuilding traditions of the East China Sea featured wooden-planked vessels with much deeper hulls. These ship hulls were U- or V-shaped and oriented around a keel, making them better suited to the transportation of larger amounts of cargo on the open sea (see Figure 12) (Kimura, 2016: 16). They also featured bulkheads, and multiple layers of planking fastened with iron nails (Figures 13–15) (Kimura, 2016: 8, 17).

Several important shipwrecks dating from the Song Dynasty have been recovered on the southern coast of China and in Southeast Asian waters. The Southern Song Nanhai I vessel was recovered just off the coast of Guangdong Province and its large hull demonstrates hallmarks of Chinese construction, including bulkheads and iron nails (Zhou et al., 2021). The cargo of the ship is still being investigated, but numerous examples of foreign goods and even foreign DNA have been recovered from the vessel (Chen, 2019). In the late Song Dynasty, a ship full of herbs, spices, and drugs was abandoned in the

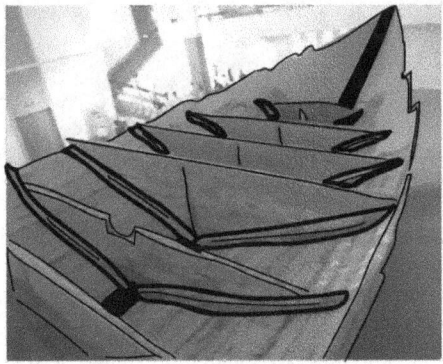

Figure 12 Visible Keel, Ribs, and Bulkheads of Quanzhou Ship, Quanzhou Maritime Museum

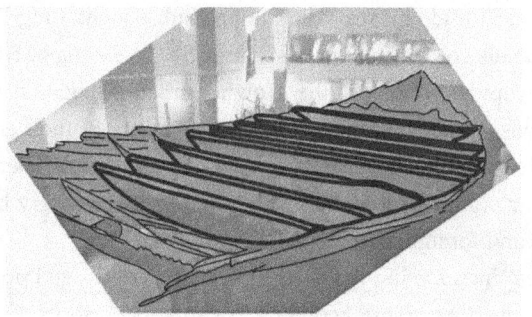

Figure 13 Bulkheads of Quanzhou Ship, Quanzhou Maritime Museum

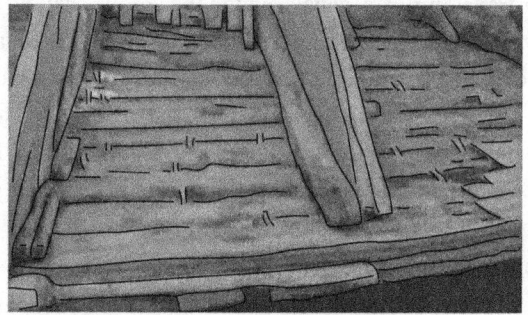

Figure 14 Quanzhou Ship Hull Planking, Fastenings, Ribs, and Bulkhead, Quanzhou Maritime Museum

Figure 15 Quanzhou Ship Plank Fastenings, Ribs, and Bulkhead, Quanzhou Maritime Museum

harbor of the Fujian port city of Quanzhou where it was covered over by sediment which preserved much of its contents (see Figures 16 and 17) (Pearson et al., 2002: 46; Kimura, 2016: 73). The Quanzhou ship was buried

Figure 16 The Quanzhou Ship Hull, Quanzhou Maritime Museum

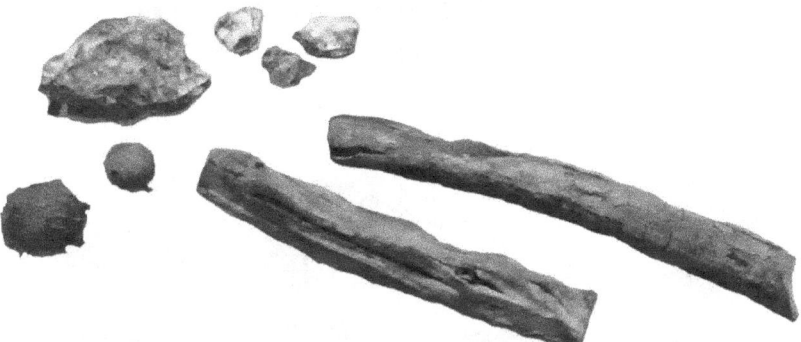

Figure 17 Spices and incense recovered from the Quanzhou Ship, Quanzhou Maritime Museum

while holding a cargo that included sandalwood, agarwood, pepper, frankincense, betel nuts, ambergris, cinnabar, mercury, multiple storage jars and a wooden container, and 94 wooden product labels (Kimura, 2016: Appendix I). These materials speak to the robust long-distance exchange of spices and medicines between China, Southeast Asia, South Asia, and the Middle East during the Global Middle Ages.

The structure of the Quanzhou ship included the primary features of shipbuilding in the East China Sea region, and the circumstances of its loss in the harbor preserved evidence of many details of its construction (see Figure 18). The hull remains are 24.2 meters long and consist of a keel (called a "dragon's spine"), bulkheads, a transom stern with a rudder socket, and multiple layers of planking (see Figures 19–25) (Kimura, 2016: 74, 77–79). Green, Burningham, the Quanzhou Maritime Museum,[7] and Kimura describe the complicated style of planking in the hull as combining flush, edge-to-edge components with

---

[7] The Quanzhou Maritime Museum is "The Museum of Overseas Communication History" named in the Green et al. article.

Figure 18 Quanzhou Ship Outer Hull, Quanzhou Maritime Museum

Figure 19 Quanzhou Ship Rudder Socket and Bulkheads, Quanzhou Maritime Museum

Figure 20 Quanzhou Ship with Mast Base on Far Left, Quanzhou Maritime Museum

Global Ships 33

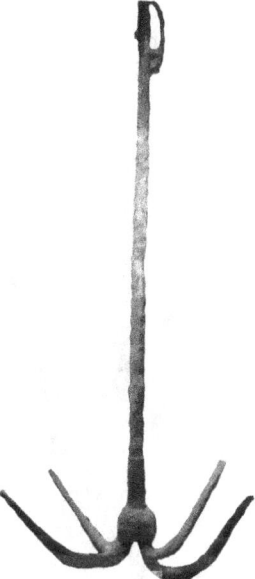

Figure 21 Quanzhou Maritime Museum Iron Anchor

Figure 22 Quanzhou Maritime Museum Grapnel Anchor

overlapped, clinker-built layers (Green et al., 1998; Kimura, 2016: 74, 83). The keel of the ship was comprised of three joined segments, and the joint between the forward and central sections contained a *bao shou kong*, or "hole for holding longevity" (Kimura, 2016: 80, 261). This ritual feature of boatbuilding in southern China involves the placement of coins in the position of the navigational constellation of the Great Bear and a mirror representing the full moon

Figure 23 Quanzhou Maritime Museum Wooden Anchor

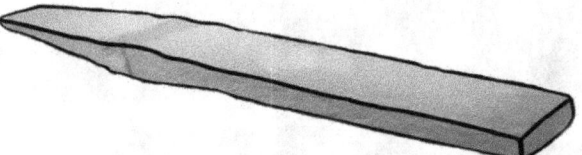

Figure 24 Quanzhou Maritime Museum Stone Anchor

directly into the spine of the ship (see Figure 26) (Kimura, 2016: 261). Cultural and religious rituals aimed at securing the safety of seafarers have been documented in boatbuilding practices in many parts of the world and speak to the lived experience of risk taken on by ships' crews and long-distance merchants.

As long-distance seafaring developed along the southern coast and shipbuilding traditions from multiple regions came into increased contact, shipbuilders in China and Southeast Asia began borrowing ideas and innovations from one another. Shipbuilding along the southern coast of China developed a hybrid approach that combined practices and technologies from the East China Sea region and Southeast Asia. Shipwrecks recovered in Southeast Asia dating from the Song Dynasty reveal a blending of shipbuilding traditions that represent intensive cultural contact between Southeast Asian and Chinese shipwrights. Manguin and Kimura have identified hybrid structural features in the south China tradition

Figure 25 Quanzhou Maritime Museum Woven Sail Model

Figure 26 Model of *Baoshu Kong* Longevity Holes, Quanzhou Maritime Museum

including the use of axial rudders and multiple layers of teak planks that are edge-joined by dowels and then attached to bulkheads using iron nails (Manguin, 2012: 184; Kimura, 2016: 9,18). Southeast Asian wrecks have combined Austronesian lashed-lug construction with bulkheads and other Chinese features.

The Java Sea shipwreck, which was recovered in Indonesian waters, points towards the cultural exchange that was occurring in the south China-Southeast Asia contact zone during the Global Middle Ages. Traveling with a cargo of diverse trade goods from China, Southeast Asia, South Asia, and Africa during the Southern Song period, the vessel's structure exhibited hybrid structural features (Mathers & Flecker, 1997: 72). Almost none of the ship survived on the seafloor, but the wreckage pattern of the heavy iron concretions onboard trace a ghost-outline of the ship's structure (Mathers & Flecker, 1997: 66). The position of the large blocks of concretions map out the sections of a cargo hold divided by bulkheads, and remaining pieces of wood from the ship's structure contain Southeast Asian-style dowel holes (Mathers & Flecker, 1997: 66–67, 69). The ship's structural remains have been identified as having been worked from species native to Southeast Asia (Mathers & Flecker, 1997: 70–71). What is clear in the case of the Java Sea wreck and other hybrid vessels populating the coasts and seafloor of the region is that technologies and seafaring practices circulated on the water just as readily as commodities and cargo. The Global Middle Ages in Chinese and Southeast Asian waters was a time of cultural exchange and technological hybridity.

The Yuan-Ming transition of the late fourteenth century witnessed a dramatic upheaval in maritime activity on China's southern coast. Foreign merchants in the port cities gained new political power under Mongol rule, but were scapegoated as collaborators during and after the transfer of power to the Ming. Many fled southern China and established communities in the port cities of Southeast Asia, thereby increasing the exchange of shipbuilding technologies between regions. Much has been written about the Ming dynasty's maritime policies of restricted foreign trade and attempts to centralize long-distance commercial relationships through the fifteenth-century voyages of the sea admiral, Zheng He. Sources dating from the late sixteenth-eighteenth centuries describe the ships in Zheng He's fleets as being impossibly large, nearly the size of one and a half American football fields, each (Church, 2005: 2, 4). The recorded size of these treasure ships has, at times, been taken literally by historians but is better understood rhetorically, in light of the context in which these accounts were written. Regardless of the size of the ships, Zheng He's voyages to Southeast Asia and across the Indian Ocean demonstrated the cosmopolitan nature of what seafaring along the southern coast of China had become over the centuries. As a Muslim sea admiral representing the interests of Ming China in far-away ports, Zheng He embodied the historical trajectory and complexity of maritime trade in China's Global Middle Ages. The mythologizing of the structure and size of his ships is also another reminder of the political stakes of accounts of maritime technology.

5 Competition and Change in the Mediterranean

Section five of Global Ships *explores shifts in the construction methods of merchant vessels in the Mediterranean from mortise-and-tenon, hull-first vessels to watercraft built from the frame outward. Oared galleys and sailing vessels from the North African coast, the Levant, the western Mediterranean, and the Black Sea plied the waters of a diverse and competitive commercial space that spanned the chronological rise and fall of multiple centers of political and economic power during the Global Middle Ages. Multiple shipwrecks document the transition that occurred in shipbuilding and rigging in the region and the rivalries that would ultimately play a role in initiating the Age of Sail.*

The eastern Mediterranean had long been connected to the trade routes of the Red Sea and Indian Ocean worlds, and during the Global Middle Ages the sea power of the western waters grew exponentially (Schoff, 1912). The Iberian ships that ultimately crossed the Atlantic and rounded the Cape of Good Hope into the Indian Ocean were the result of centuries of technological exchange and cross-cultural contact in the laboratory of the globalized Mediterranean world. The Mediterranean has produced numerous shipwrecks from different eras and subregions, and this long archive of maritime materials demonstrates the competing powers not only of empires and thalassocracies, but of the raw structuring forces of the environment and human endeavor.

The wind is a hidden driver of Mediterranean history. Seafaring in the premodern Mediterranean was a seasonal enterprise because of the volatility of winter winds and weather and the dramatic difference in visibility at different times of year. The summer wind in the eastern sea blows from the north-northwest, driving maritime traffic to the eastern littoral (Casson, 2014: 272). The patterns of dominant wind direction and water currents in the Mediterranean have privileged the eastern shores of the Levant and Egyptian coast with an advantageous position and helped to build empires and trade networks across the eastern basin. A counterclockwise sea route around the eastern littoral likely dates from the middle Bronze Age (McGrail, 2001: 112). The seasonal winds in the Aegean have structured military and trade relationships, and the mistral links the climate of the Atlantic with the western Mediterranean by blowing across the sweep of France. Desert winds from the northern coast of Africa and winds from the east within the western sea create distinct local seafaring conditions and delineate maritime subregions in the broader Mediterranean.

Ancient Greeks and Romans limited seafaring to summer because of the dangers of limited visibility outside of the sailing season, and ancient approaches to boatbuilding reflected the reality that up to 20 percent of the days of the seafaring season have little to no wind (McGrail, 2001: 92; Casson, 2014: 270–271). Boats require propulsion to move across the water, and in the context of premodern seafaring that meant utilizing the power of the wind or of human strength through rowing. With a sailing season of sometimes unreliable winds, shipbuilding traditions in the Mediterranean utilized both human strength and the wind, in the form of square sails and/or banks of oarsmen.

Before the second millennium BCE, shipbuilding throughout the Mediterranean featured sewn-boat construction (McGrail, 2001: 145–147). The impact of the relationship between premodern Egypt and the cultures of the eastern seacoast cannot be overstated in terms of its influence on boatbuilding across the entire Mediterranean region. The development of the mortise-and-tenon joint in this contact zone would shape construction practices throughout the sea. Regular exchange of maritime technologies and materials led to a set of shipbuilding practices that would persist well into the Global Middle Ages (McGrail, 2001: 106). The Mediterranean's role as a nexus of intersecting contact zones would shape its trajectory as traditional construction methods from the Egyptian-Red Sea-Indian Ocean, Levantine, North African, Aegean-Black Sea, and western sea-Atlantic Ocean contact regions hybridized into new forms.

Hull-first construction methods utilizing sewing, treenails, and/or mortise-and-tenon joints were dominant across the region during the rise and fall of numerous sea powers (McGrail, 2001: 138). Locked mortise-and-tenon joints, known as Phoenician joints by the Romans, possessed real advantages for naval warfare by increasing the structural stability of vessels in the event of ramming (McGrail, 2001: 133, 148). The cargo of the wreck of the Rochelongue ship in the western sea demonstrates the expansive activity of Phoenician merchants across the Mediterranean in the Iron Age. Etruscan, Greek, and Phoenician metals and artifacts were recovered at the wreck site off the southwestern coast of France dating from the sixth to seventh century BCE (Aragon, 2018: 39, 41). Phoenician maritime activities bridged the tumultuous conclusion of the Bronze Age with renewed Iron Age prosperity and the changing political configurations in the Mediterranean during Antiquity. The geographic scope of their trade and navigational activities was immense. Researchers have detected the chemical biomarker for cinnamon[8] from South or Southeast Asia inside ten Phoenician-made clay flasks excavated in Israel that date from the tenth to eleventh centuries BCE, demonstrating direct links between Levantine trade networks with those of the Indian Ocean at a very early date (Gilboa & Namdar, 2015: 269, 270, 273–274). Radiographic and botanical analysis of the remains of

---

[8] Cinnamaldehyde.

Ramesses II, roughly a century earlier, identified Indian black pepper in his abdominal and nasal cavities from the mummification process and Egyptian sources from the second millennium BCE discuss the spice trade with Punt and Asia (Lichtenberg & Thuilliez, 1981; Plu, 1985: 174; Gilboa & Namdar, 2015: 272). Remains of Chinese cassia flower have been identified in a temple context in the eastern Aegean dating from the seventh century BCE, and Near Eastern and Greek sources discuss the local presence of Asian spices in this period (Gilboa & Namdar, 2015: 272, 274–275). These archaeological and textual findings provide an important backdrop for understanding the development of the spice trade in later eras, up to and beyond the Global Middle Ages.

In Antiquity, Herodotus reports that the navigational abilities of the Phoenicians led them beyond the Mediterranean into the Atlantic Ocean and, though he dismisses aspects of the reports of their circumnavigation of Africa, the details he preserved in his account have caused modern scholars to engage with these claims more seriously[9] (Herodotus, 1921: 239–241, 399; Kahanov, 2000: 66). Western historiography has long been embedded in contests of imperial or state power, and this narrative lineage began with Herodotus' accounts of Persian power in the eastern Mediterranean. Narratives of difference emergent from the Greco-Persian wars make it difficult to characterize cosmopolitan, and often overlapping, technologies at sea in Antiquity. The discipline of history has traditionally given greater weight to political rivalries and tensions that produce territorial conflicts and nationalistic conceptions of place, environment, and technology than to connection. The fluidity of the water has been offered by more recent scholars as an alternative analytical framework to war for thinking about connectivity and exchange. But the role of shipbuilding technology in the historiography of the Mediterranean navigates a narrative Scylla and Charybdis when it comes to warfare. On the one side, scholars must maneuver around the dangers of an inherited hyper-focus on military history to the exclusion of other seagoing activities and on the other, must navigate the risk of neglecting the profound influence of conflict on seafaring in an attempt to highlight connectivity. Both narrative hazards must be avoided. Although the maritime historiography of previous generations was largely restricted to military contests and conquests and newer approaches to oceanic studies present the opportunity to understand exchange and contact, it is important to recognize that the fluidity of the world's oceans has been a site of enormous competition as well as synthesis. As a discursive space, conflict in the Mediterranean region was the propulsive force in the sails of Orientalist civilizational narratives that have shaped Eurocentric

---

[9] See Herodotus, *The Histories*, 4.42 & 4.198.

periodizations of the past and formed the basis of the historiographic structures the Global Middle Ages analytic seeks to disrupt.

The Aegean, Bosporus, Black Sea, Levant, and North African coasts share a heritage of war vessels powered by seated banks of rowers. Biremes and triremes structurally supported the work of large numbers of oarsmen because the sometimes unreliable or unavailable wind did not meet the urgent needs of battle (Casson, 2014). Oared galleys with square sails and locked mortise-and-tenon construction came to dominate the eastern and central Mediterranean over time (McGrail, 2001: 141). In the first millennium BCE, sewing was still used to bolster vulnerable areas of locked mortise-and-tenon boats, but metal nails came into increasing use (McGrail, 2001: 147).

As Rome rose as a sea power it spread lasting traditions adopted from the Hellenistic Mediterranean and appropriated boat-building cultures from across its expanding empire (McGrail, 2001: 154). Mediterranean-style boats made from local wood have been recovered in Britain dating from 290 to 300 CE (McGrail, 2001: 194). A hybrid Celtic-Roman shipbuilding tradition emerged from the contact of empire that featured more heavily framed boats that were assembled with large iron nails (McGrail, 2001: 196–197). Maritime scholars have speculated that the transmission of this new hybrid tradition back to the Mediterranean may have eventually stimulated the development of frame-first, rather than hull-first, construction methods (McGrail, 2001: 205).

The increasing size of grain and cargo ships also contributed to the use of wooden framing in more structurally critical ways. The turn of the millennium saw the development of merchant ships of growing size with large-capacity hulls that were double-planked (McGrail, 2001: 155–157). The framing built inside these vessels became more important to supporting the structures of the hull, though it remained a secondary step to the planking of the boat's shell in the building process (McGrail, 2001: 163). A large merchant vessel from this period known as the Kefalonia/Fiscardo shipwreck was found in the Ionian Sea and ships of similar large capacity, up to 400 tons, have also been found in France, Italy, and Tunisia (Ferentinos G. et al., 2020).

Two Byzantine ships recovered from the same area in Turkish waters represent the dramatic changes that occurred in Mediterranean shipbuilding during the Global Middle Ages. The first wreck, the Yassi Ada II, was a small cargo ship that sank in the fourth century CE and reflected the traditional approach to shipbuilding. The construction used mortise-and-tenon joints and was built hull-first (McGrail, 2001: 158–159). The second wreck, the Yassi Ada I, was built c. 625 CE and demonstrates the dynamic shifts in construction witnessed in this period. The ship had a unique build that combined a hull-first approach to construction below the water line with frame-first methods above (McGrail, 2001: 162). Significantly, though it is challenging to accurately identify the early use of lateen sails using shipwreck remains, maritime archaeologist J. Richard Steffy has identified adaptations to the ship's rigging that could indicate the presence of lateen sails (Steffy, 1982; McGrail, 2001: 159).

Examples of mixed construction methods with a more progressively active role for framing are noted in the archaeological record of late Antiquity and the early Middle Ages (Pomey et al., 2012). The seventh–eleventh centuries CE witnessed the transition from plank-first, hull-first construction to frame-first methods across the Mediterranean, with early examples found in wrecks from Israel, France, and Sicily (McGrail, 2001: 158, 161). Possible reasons for this change have been suggested by many, including economic advantages given the reduced labor and time required for this new approach that lacked elaborate plank fastenings and wood carving (McGrail, 2001: 158). Environmental and social factors related to the reduced availability of trees for ship construction have also been proposed (Pomey et al., 2012: 236). The 1025 CE Byzantine merchant wreck known as the Serçe Limanı I was built entirely frame-first, without mortise-and-tenon or sewn plank fastenings (McGrail, 2001: 161–163; Pomey et al., 2012: 277). This holotype would become the dominant variety of ship sailing in Mediterranean waters.

The new frame-first approach to construction in the Mediterranean was not only more economical from the standpoint of labor, time, and timber, but enabled the building of larger hulls that were better equipped for longer journeys at sea (McGrail, 2001: 164). Venice emerged as a center of frame-first boat design and construction in the Global Middle Ages, and Venetian shipbuilding manuscripts have been an important source of information on late medieval and early modern seafaring (McGrail, 2001: 165; Campana, 2009; Bondioli, 2017). Venetian texts from the fourteenth and fifteenth centuries include instructions for piloting ships, using equipment and rigging, and proportions for the construction of round ships (Bondioli, 2017: 216). A derelict Venetian galley and flat-bottomed cargo vessel that were submerged in the Venice lagoon at San Marco in Boccalama were investigated in 2001 and dated to the early fourteenth century by dendrochronology and radiocarbon analysis (D'Agostino & Medas, 2003). Scratched into the interior hull of the galley are graffiti drawings, ostensibly made by the crew, or possibly in a shipyard. The most prominent of these drawings is of a trireme with a stern-mounted rudder and rigging, and this relatable doodle of the past inside the hull of the ship is powerful evidence today of lives lived at sea (D'Agostino & Medas, 2003: 25). The derelict ship is the first galley ever found by archaeologists in the Mediterranean. A *fusta*, which is a smaller oared craft, has also been found in Lake Garda and a Catalonian round ship was recovered dating from the fourteenth century (D'Agostino & Medas, 2003: 26). Shipwrecks in the Mediterranean, or made there, become more frequent finds beginning from the sixteenth century onward.

Merchant cities divided the shipbuilding process into specialized divisions of labor that sped up the production timeline. As Venetian and Genoese ships in the thirteenth century connected the central Mediterranean with Islamic Spain and the Atlantic to the west and Alexandria, the Levant, and the Black Sea to the east, multiple shipbuilding practices once again came into direct contact (Castro, 2008: 75, 79). A fifteenth-century Mamluk shipwreck was reported by Israel's Antiquities Authority at the port of Caesarea in 2021 and recent Ottoman finds in the Black Sea and eastern Mediterranean demonstrate the promise of ongoing archaeological recovery, despite the threats presented by looters (The Guardian, 2021; Garbov & Batchvarov, 2022; DAMTCW, 2022). The Global Middle Ages was a period of technological contact, and ultimately, transformation in the Mediterranean, and continued research into maritime archaeology in this important contact zone will no doubt shed greater light on the history of global seafaring.

6 Viking Ships and Trade Vessels in Northern and Western Europe

In section six of Global Ships, the diffusion of clinker-constructed Viking vessels in the North Sea, the Baltic, and across the northern Atlantic is explored in relationship to other ship structures in Europe. Longships and cargo vessels are examined alongside the development of the hulc and cog. Important sources for understanding these ships are explored in the remains of the Oseberg and Gokstad boat burials in Norway and the Skuldelev shipwrecks in Denmark.

The reach of the globalism of the Viking voyages and culture has been revisited in recent research that reflects the diverse genetic origins of Viking society (Margaryan et al., 2020). Despite its geographic (and oceanic) cosmopolitan reach, spanning from North America to Iran, Viking culture has been deployed in discourses of White supremacy from the nineteenth century to the present day as a purity-phantasm of the racist imagination (Gabriele, 2021). Vikings and Viking shipbuilding, in particular, play a tripart role in the development of Eurocentric narratives of seafaring that link Whiteness to technological superiority. First, as the early pioneers of Atlantic crossings who sailed from Europe to North America centuries before Columbus, their westward journeys are framed as a fateful foreshadowing of manifest destiny and European colonial occupation of the Americas (Mancini, 2002). Second, components of their seafaring technology influenced the structures of the hybrid ships of Columbus and later European explorers, and third, a great deal of research carried out on their boats and burials was conducted by Nazi archaeologists, who contributed to the construction of the pseudo-history of their Whiteness (Parry, 1951/1952: 26; Scott, 1996).

The Baltic and North Seas are the relatively shallow, eastern edge of the European North Atlantic region. Their cold northern climate dictates a summer sailing season and the Baltic's sheltered position eliminates the majority of tidal currents in the water[10] (McGrail, 2001: 166). The technology of Viking seafaring that emerged in this environment during the Global Middle Ages has been profoundly politicized since the archaeological excavations of boat burial mounds in Scandinavia began. This section of *Global Ships* considers the evidence recovered from major Viking burial mounds and shipwrecks in light of the archaeological climate of the nineteenth century.

Boats in the Baltic and North Seas were exclusively propelled by the power of oarsmen before the seventh century CE, when the first evidence of sails in the region appears (Crumlin-Pedersen, 1990). Nordic ships were built shell-first, using overlapping, sewn planks that were additionally fastened with iron nails by the late Roman period. Overlapping hull planking, known as clinker construction, became characteristic of ships built in Scandinavia in the centuries that followed (see Figure 27). The Swedish Bjorke ship, dated from between the fourth and sixth centuries CE, is the first extant clinker ship with all-nailed planking, though the vessel's framing was still lashed (McGrail, 2001: 208).

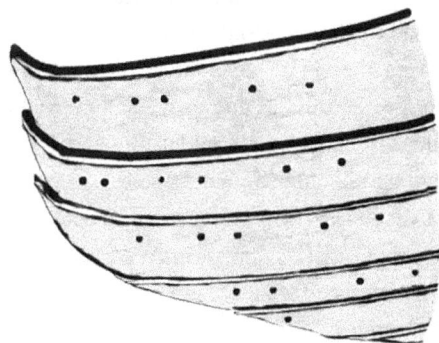

Figure 27 Overlapping, clinker-built hull construction.

---

[10] Swedish Meteorological and Hydrological Institute. (2014) Tides, www.smhi.se/en/theme/tides-1.11272#:~:text=The%20Baltic%20Sea%20is%20itself,tide%20in%20the%20Southern%20Baltic.

Crumlin-Pedersen, Westerdahl, and McGrail have argued that the shift from predominantly oar-powered to wind-powered boats in the North Sea and Baltic region occurred in tandem with increased royal control of coastal waters. As landings became safer, ship crews did not need the defensive manpower of large groups of oarsmen (Westerdahl, 1995: 41–50; Crumlin-Pedersen, 1997; McGrail, 2001: 212). This period of greater security also saw increases in boat size and shipping capacity, as well as the development of larger vessels used for exploration and conquest.

The Scandinavian or Viking Expansion in the ninth-eleventh centuries CE saw outbound journeys originating in the Baltic and North Seas and the North Atlantic cross the waters of northern Europe and establish settlements as far away as Spain, the inner Mediterranean and Black Sea, Greenland, and North America (Greenhill & Morrison, 1995: 194). The ninth-century Gokstad ship, which was excavated in Norway, was a burial vessel with a light, oak-planked hull and was the largest Viking ship ever found. The clinker-built vessel supported thirty-two oarsmen and had strong mast support for sailing. The ship's radiocarbon dating places its construction at around 895 CE (Greenhill & Morrison, 1995: 197; McGrail, 2001: 212, 217).

The ornate, clinker-built, Oseberg burial ship in Norway is slightly older than the Gokstad vessel but also dates from the ninth century. The ship was utilized in the elaborate ritual burial of two elite women (Greenhill & Morrison, 1995: 196; McGrail, 2001: 214). Though the ship dates from c. 815–820 CE, its burial near inland, sheltered waters and the creation of the interment mound date from 834 CE (Greenleaf & Morrison, 1995: 196; McGrail, 2001: 212). The high status of the women buried at Oseberg has yielded an enormous amount of evidence about the long-distance trade of luxury goods in the Viking period of migration. Silk textiles recovered from the burial have shed new light in recent years on the connections that Nordic elites in the Viking age enjoyed with the East. Marianne Vedeler's work at the Museum of Cultural History at the University of Oslo has breathed new life into the silk finds from the Oseberg ship burial, which were first excavated in 1904 (Vedeler, 2014: 3). Numerous Byzantine, Central Asian, and Persian silk threads, embroideries, and strips were recovered from the site and Vedeler documents the presence of older Sasanian patterns still in circulation after the seventh-century conquest of Iran in the assemblage (Vedeler, 2014: 14).

A wooden bucket adorned with a brass and cloisonné figure resembling the seated Buddha in meditation, surrounded by Buddhist-appearing swastika symbols, was also recovered from the burial, and has raised heated debate on the nature and possibility of cultural contact between the Vikings and Silk Road cultures in the ninth century (Burge, 2021: 29). Unfortunately, the twentieth-century framing of this conversation seems to miss the anthropological complexity of artistic exchange and the construction of hybrid cultural objects that is part and parcel to the material culture of trade routes and seafaring. Discussions of the artifact are often buried in reductionist binaries of *whose* culture the object represents, rather than an analysis of how cultures interact and produce new meanings. Because the Oseberg site was excavated just a year before Norway's independence, the ship and its Viking heritage have taken on a pointedly nationalistic symbolism (Scott, 1996: 325). The emergence of Nazi archaeology in the decades after the recovery of the Oseberg vessel saw SS sponsorship of Viking site excavations, and the development of a racist official narrative anointing Viking ships as symbols of so-called Aryan origins. Scandinavian archaeologists who resisted this development were imprisoned and suppressed (Scott, 1996: 332–333). Ongoing research on non-local materials, inscriptions, and artistic motifs found in Viking-age boat graves can be further contextualized by emerging genetic research revealing the diversity and long-distance connections woven into Scandinavia's past (Wärmländer et al., 2015; Samuel, 2017; Larsson, 2020: 123; Rodríguez-Varela et al., 2023). For example, the remains of one of the women interred in the Oseberg ship have been identified as belonging to a DNA haplogroup associated with Iranian or Black Sea heritage (Holck, 2006: 185). Future research on Viking society within the historical context of a cosmopolitan Global Middle Ages will further elaborate the networks of connection that informed Scandinavian seafaring.

The ninth–tenth century Klåstad cargo vessel was constructed with a deeper hull than the Gokstad or Oseberg ships and was built with a tree-nailed frame without lashes (McGrail, 2001: 217). McGrail has traced similar changes in hull depth and shape in other vessels featuring a more V-shaped orientation around a keel and stronger framing support that allowed for larger cargo capacity (McGrail, 2001: 215, 217). In the eleventh century, a small group of Viking ships was intentionally sunk to the bottom of a channel at Skuldelev, near Copenhagen, to block the passage of invaders (Greenleaf & Morrison, 1995: 200; McGrail, 2001: 223).[11] The assemblage contains multiple ship types, including a raiding longship and a cargo vessel (Greenleaf & Morrison, 1995: 200). These wrecks are significant as the first major find of Viking ships from a non-burial context. The cargo vessel, a ship-type known as a keel, had a capacity of twenty-five tons (Castro, 2008: 72).

Castro has argued that the Viking cargo ships of the era of the Skuldelev find are the predecessors of the double-ended, clinker-built, medieval hulc vessel, which is known only through iconographic and textual evidence rather than

---

[11] The Viking Museum (2016). *The five Viking ships – The Skuldelev Ships*, www.vikingeskibsmuseet.dk/en/visit-the-museum/exhibitions/the-five-viking-ships.

through archaeological finds (Castro, 2008: 72). The lack of archaeological evidence for hulcs has presented a challenge for understanding the complex technological relationships between medieval boatbuilding traditions in European waters. Iconographic representations of hulcs featured classic aspects of Viking ship-design with the addition of structural castles above the main deck and a more flattened hull. Recent investigations of a large, medieval, clinker-built shipwreck with a forecastle in the waters of the Stockholm archipelago have reignited hopes for the possibility of clear material evidence of the hulc. Radiocarbon wiggle-matching analysis conducted on the wreck's timbers dates the ship to 1492–1503 (Ericksson, 2021: 116, 121).

Nordic ships in the Viking age featured double-ended construction and a single, central mast with a square sail, but the introduction of the stern rudder around 1200 CE led to a change in hull form and differentiation between the bow and stern. The typically flat-bottomed, double-ended, single-masted cog ship came to dominate the North Sea and Baltic in the thirteenth and fourteenth centuries (McGrail, 2001: 232–234). By this period, larger cargo holds facilitated increased trade and McGrail has argued that these changes were driven by increased economic contact and competition (McGrail, 2001: 231–232). Hulcs and keels competed with cogs along the coasts of northwestern Europe, and as in other maritime contact zones in the Global Middle Ages, new hybrid ship forms were the result (McGrail, 2001: 232; Eriksson, 2021: 125). Keels gradually disappeared, and Henry V's 1418 Grace Dieu ship is, at present, the last-excavated large Nordic ship (McGrail, 2001: 232). A ship known as the Bremen cog was discovered in Bremerhaven in the 1960s that has been used as a kind of archaeological holotype for interpreting textual, iconographic, and wreckage related to the development of the cog in the late Middle Ages (Eriksson, 2021: 125). Interestingly, unlike hulcs or keels, cogs used hooked-iron nails seen in earlier Celtic-Roman vessels (Ellmers 1990 in McGrail, 2001: 221). Cogs were also heavier-framed ships than keels, and McGrail has argued that this may represent continuity with Celtic-Roman boatbuilding traditions (McGrail, 2001: 239).

The fourteenth century was an era of enhanced contact between cogs from the North Sea and Baltic region and frame-first constructed galleys from the Mediterranean. Cogs made their way into the Mediterranean and Genoese and Venetian merchants made their way into northern harbors. The larger cargo capacity of cogs influenced Venetian and other regional shipbuilders in this period to redesign their cargo ships (McGrail, 2001: 243–244). The Mediterranean construction of cogs began in Genoa, Venice, and Catalonia, but instead of using the northern shell-first approach, Mediterranean shipwrights built them frame-first, like their galleys. These Mediterranean frame-first cogs were called *cocha*, and lateen sails and topsails were soon added to their rigging (McGrail, 2001: 244). Images of three-masted ships that included square and lateen sails appear in European charts and art from 1350 CE, then more frequently in the fifteenth century (Greenleaf & Morrison, 1995: 258–259). Though northern shipwrights did not apply Mediterranean frame-first methods to the construction of their own cogs, McGrail argues that they did come to prefer the cost-effective hulc, which could be built much faster than a cog, by the mid fifteenth century (McGrail, 2001: 240).

The cog-inspired, frame-first *cocha* became a critical player in Mediterranean merchant networks in just a matter of decades. A three-masted *cocha* first appears in a Catalonian illustration in 1406, and in northern waters the *cocha* became known as the carrack, the vessel-type of Columbus' flagship, the *Santa María* (Astengo, 1992: 438; McGrail, 2001: 232–234, 244–245). Viking and Mediterranean shipbuilding methods merged in the shipyards of the late Global Middle Ages, and hybridizing not only their own local traditions, but the far-flung technologies that had come to inform their ships for centuries. By the time of its emergence, the carrack was a hybrid of components from Asia, the Islamicate world, the Mediterranean, and the Viking contact zone.

7 Weaponized Ships

Section seven of Global Ships *traces the increased weaponization of merchant vessels associated with European navigation of the Indian Ocean and Atlantic up to the year 1500. Gradual shifts in the construction of seafaring ships to accommodate increased firepower in the fourteenth and fifteenth centuries became a hallmark of Iberian voyages of conquest. The historical, structural relationships between warships and merchant vessels and the development of the carrack (*nau*), and galleon are discussed in light of the development of maritime firepower in East and Southeast Asia. The structural transformation of ships into slavers and the narrative weaponization of European shipbuilding in colonial discourse conclude a discussion of the changing nature of contact at sea in the twilight of the Global Middle Ages.*

The final section of this study will consider the weaponization of the boats of the Global Middle Ages in three intersecting arenas: first, through the increased physical armament of ships, second, through an examination of the structural changes made to vessels to accommodate the use of gunpowder weapons and the early facilitation of the slave trade, and finally, in discursive representations of the ships of European colonial contact and conquest.

Despite the technological chauvinism of colonial discourse about sea power—gunpowder, bombs, and firearms unequivocally began as Asian technologies.

As recipes for gunpowder and weapons technology spread from East Asia across the trade routes and through the conquests of Mongol empire, maritime cultures across Afro-Eurasia adopted and adapted these new weapons to their own seafaring contexts and cultures.

The adoption of onboard gunpowder weapons and artillery can first be traced through the wreckage of shipwrecks in East and Southeast Asia. After its invention in China, gunpowder was first used in warfare during the Song dynasty (960–1279 CE) (Sinvany, 2019: 2–3). Stoneware bombs, the oldest gunpowder weapons recovered from shipwrecks anywhere in the world (to date), were excavated from the wreckage of the second attempted Mongol invasion of Japan in 1281 (see Figure 28) (Ikeda et al., 2019). A cannon, iron gun, and stone cannon balls have also been recovered from the Penglai shipwreck site in China dating from the late Yuan and early Ming periods (Liang & Wang, 2022: 54–55, 64).

Numerous gunpowder weapons and cannons have been recovered from shipwreck sites in Southeast Asia dating from the fifteenth century. Several firearms were recovered from the Maranei wreck of a Chinese smuggler in Indonesian waters dating from between 1401 and 1424 CE. Two firearms were recovered from the c. 1460–1500 CE Pandanan wreck of a Southeast Asian ship in the Philippines, and five other firearms were found in the Philippines in the wreckage of the Ming dynasty Lena Shoal wreck, c. 1490–1500 CE (Brown, 2004: 53). The Brunei Junk (c.1505 CE) yielded seven additional firearms, and Roxana Brown has described three additional firearms being excavated in an unpublished wreck in the region.

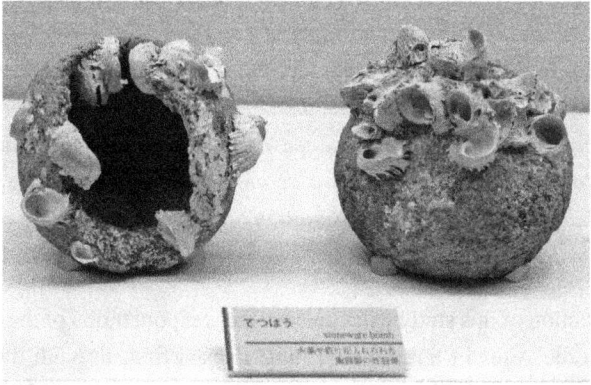

Figure 28 Takashima Shipwreck stoneware bomb, Japan. Modified from the original by 震天動地 (https://commons.wikimedia.org/wiki/File:%E3%81%A6%E3%81%A4%E3%81%AF%E3%81%86%EF%BC%88%E9%9 C%87%E5%A4%A9%E9%9B%B7%EF%BC%89.JPG) used under CC BY-SA 3.0 (https://creativecommons.org/licenses/by-sa/3.0).

Brown makes the important point that all of these materials predate the Portuguese invasion of Malacca in 1511 (Brown, 2004: 53).

Changes to boat forms in Europe that saw the addition of castles above the main decks of ships had allowed for competing parties in the North Sea and Baltic to use height to their advantage to rain (traditional) fire on their enemies (Eriksson, 2021: 127). Battles between and within the Kalmar Union and Hanseatic League were staged on the castles of hulcs and cogs, which were used as tactical fighting platforms. Crossbows and other weapons on the attack from above could do significant damage to an opposing crew with little direct face-to-face contact (Eriksson, 2021: 127).

The Mediterranean was no stranger to weaponized hulls, with rams built into the bodies of galleys from Antiquity. Catapults and wooden tubes lined with bronze were used to deliver the deadly "Greek fire" from the decks of Byzantine dromons (Casson, 2014: 152–153). The arrival of gunpowder weapons and the increasing presence of fore and aft castles on large ships was a potent technological combination. Small arms and falconets were added to crossbows and the traditional artillery of European ships, and increasingly heavy cannons were used on the main deck, which caused hazards to the ship's stability. Safety was improved with the addition of a gundeck below the main deck to house heavier cannons, and guns blazing from this new, lowered level meant unprecedented catastrophe for the hulls of targeted ships (Edwards, 1992: 448).

The carrack, with its hybrid Mediterranean and potentially Celtic-Roman inspired frame and northern hull capacity has been described as a "floating fortress" for its castles and its onboard artillery and ordnance (Astengo, 1992: 438–439). Carracks with large fore and aft castles and a cargo capacity of more than 700 tons have been described, along with the Portuguese caravel, as the European "protagonists of oceanic voyages, and of sailing techniques" (Astengo, 1992: 437–438). This dramatic framing of the hero story of the birth of Modernity sets shipbuilding in the Iberian peninsula as the scene. Known as *caraccas* or *naus* in the Iberian Peninsula, the rigging of the carrack combined the square sail of the ancient Mediterranean and Viking ships with the lateen sail of the Indian Ocean (see Figure 29). Greenleaf and Morrison have called these vessels the "tool of the European expansion" and Astengo argues that the "strategically located Iberian peninsula was the nexus of two worlds," in its position between the Mediterranean and the Atlantic (Astengo, 1992: 73; Greenleaf & Morrison, 1995: 259). But, the Iberian peninsula was not the nexus of two worlds, it was the nexus of at least three. Centuries of Muslim rule and cultural production in Islamic Spain had facilitated a cosmopolitan environment for the exchange of technologies and ideas during the Global Middle Ages. Even in the very moment at the close of the fifteenth century

Figure 29 A *nau* or carrack

when Muslims and Jews were expelled from its borders, Spain continued to benefit from their technology.

The caravel, from the Portuguese *caravela*, was a fishing vessel used for exploratory expeditions of the coast (Greenleaf & Morrison, 1995: 260; McGrail, 2001: 245). Its design and lateen rigging made it better at navigating the wind than any other ship sailing the Mediterranean (Astengo, 1992: 438). The carrack and the caravel would comprise the mini-fleet sailed by Columbus across the Atlantic, and the advantages of their respective forms were eventually merged in the development of the galleon (Edward, 1992: 448). The galleon would become the workhorse of European colonialism across the planet over the subsequent centuries.

The Portuguese caravel of the late-fifteenth century initiated the first raids of the transatlantic slave trade on the African coast. Maritime human trafficking had occurred throughout the Global Middle Ages, likely in most of the ship varieties discussed in this study, but never on the scale that would come to define the Middle Passage. Growing international scholarship on the archaeological recovery and material culture of slave ships promises to expand on what we have learned from the excavation of slave ships from the seventeenth to nineteenth centuries, including the Henrietta Marie, São José, and Clotilda (see Figure 30) (Jones, 2023). Increasing finds of weaponized ships from the fifteenth and sixteenth centuries will explicate the continuities with the past represented in the form and functions of these vessels, and their terrible and impactful discontinuities.

The carracks, caravels, and galleons that sliced the world in two were each a nexus of multiple worlds that came together in the Global Middle Ages in an exchange of technology that shapes the structures of our lives today. Uncovering the remains of the global maritime past disrupts and illuminates those structures.

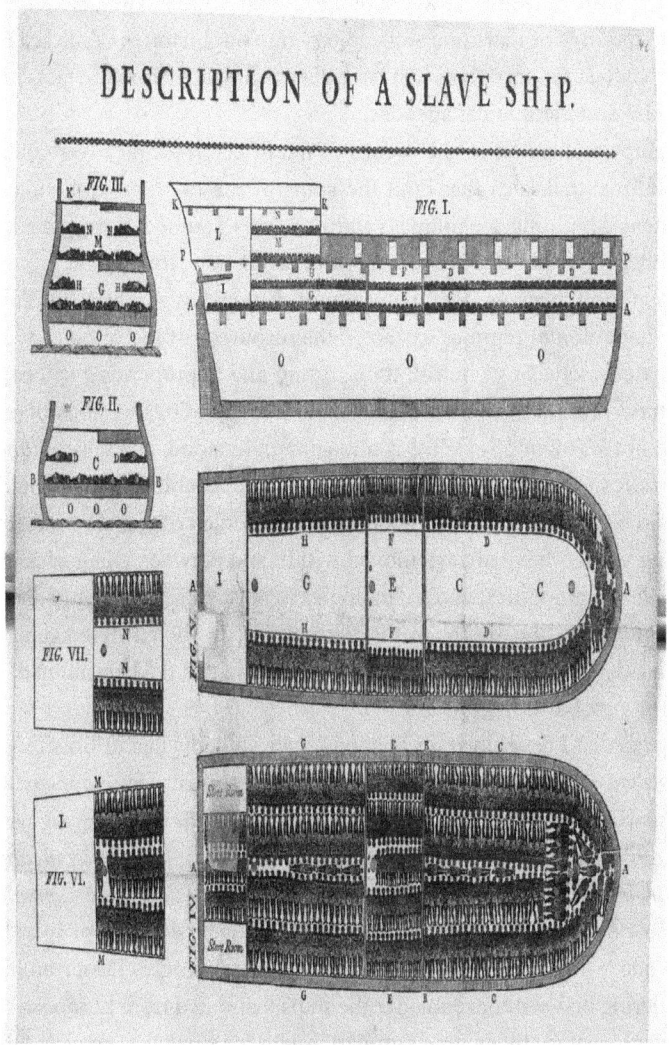

Figure 30 "The History of the Rise, Progress, and Accomplishment of the Abolition of the African Slave-Trade by the British Parliament." Thomas Clarkson. [British Library 522.f.23] Public Domain.

Conclusion

In addition to serving as an introductory survey of major premodern maritime technologies across Afro-Eurasia, this study has also been an invitation to think with, and teach with, the materials of the sea. This *Element* is an argument for understanding shipwreck materials as an archive that can be read alongside traditional textual sources to more fully understand the historical actors who moved through and built the world of the Global Middle Ages. Better incorporating the findings of maritime archaeology into our histories of the sea provides physical ballast for narratives that have departed wildly from the facts in service of colonial and ideological agendas.

The ships that sailed on the oceans of the fifteenth century were indebted to the global technologies that built the ships of the previous millennium. Hull components, building techniques, and materials sourced from generations of boatbuilders across Afro-Eurasia combined in new forms that by the early modern period became the mainstay of European colonialism. It is well known that colonial regimes extracted the resources of the regions over which they exerted increasing control, transporting and appropriating spices, timber, agricultural products, precious metals, and human beings in ships that became the workhorses of empire. What is often not understood, and what *Global Ships* demonstrates, is that the first appropriations which enabled all that would follow were of the technological components of the bodies of the ships, themselves. Seafaring vessels have always moved within and between categories, mobilizing people, commodities, and technologies in networks of exchange that disrupt the categories on the shore. In their structures, in their rigging, and in their functions, the ships that marked the end of one era and the beginning of another were, truly, global ships.

A course that I developed for undergraduate students that utilizes the material in this *Element* begins the semester with the questions: *what happens when we study the world from the standpoint of the oceans? How can studying waterways impact our understanding of history? And what can we learn, specifically, about the environment and cultural exchange from the structures and technologies of premodern boats?* Materiality matters, and our understanding of world history shifts when we include objects, artifacts, and technologies in our archives. By reconsidering how we conceptualize the ships that sailed from European shores in the fifteenth century by gaining familiarity with the ships that preceded them, the dividing lines between modernity and premodernity blur, as do the dividing lines between people that the maritime historiography of previous generations devised.

Shipwreck artifacts are often encrusted with the residue of marine life, having become the habitat of generations of creatures who utilized them during their stay underwater. But when you look underneath the residue of the intervening centuries, you are brought face-to-face with the people who built the ships of the past and produced objects, packing them, along with their hopes, into vessels that carried their traces to the present. The timbers, anchors, and structures of the ships of the Global Middle Ages that have survived underwater tell a story about the exchange of technologies between societies and the innovation of new, hybrid methods of connection across the water.

References

Abu-Lughod, J. (1989). *Before European Hegemony.* Oxford: Oxford University Press.

Agius, D. A. (2005). *Seafaring in the Arabian Gulf and Oman: The People of the Dhow.* London: Kegan Paul.

Agius, D. A. (2008). *Classic Ships of Islam: From Mesopotamia to the Indian Ocean.* Leiden: Brill.

Alexander, J. (2010). Islam, Archaeology and Slavery in Africa. *World Archaeology* 33(1), pp. 44–60.

Alpers, E. A. (2002). "Imagining the Indian Ocean World." Opening Address to the International Conference on Cultural Exchange and Transformation in the Indian Ocean World, University of California, Los Angeles, April 5–6.

Alpers, E. A. (2013). On Becoming a British Lake: Piracy, Slaving, and British Imperialism in the Indian Ocean during the First Half of the Nineteenth Century. In *Indian Ocean Slavery in the Age of Abolition.* R. Harms, B. K. Freamon, and D. W. Blight, eds. New Haven: Yale University Press, pp. 45–60.

Alpers, E. A. (2014). *The Indian Ocean in World History.* Oxford: Oxford University Press.

Anderson, A. and O'Connor, S. (2008). Indo-Pacific Migration and Colonization – Introduction. *Asian Perspectives* 47(1), pp. 2–11.

Aragon, E. (2018). The Rochelongue Underwater Site: (Re)assembling Contacts and Connectivity through a Multi-Methods Approach. In *Archaeology: Just Add Water: Underwater Research at the University of Warsaw.* A. Chołuj, M. Mileszczyk, and K. Trusz, eds. Warsaw: University of Warsaw, pp. 39–62.

Armitage, D. (1992). Christopher Columbus and the Uses of History. *History Today* 42(5), pp. 50–55.

Armitage, D. and Braddick, M. J. (2002). *The British Atlantic World, 1500–1800.* Basingstoke: Palgrave Macmillan.

Astengo, C. (1992). The State of European Science and Technology in the Late Middle Ages. *GeoJournal* 26(4), pp. 437–442.

Bass, G. F. (1986). A Bronze Age Shipwreck at Ulu Burun (Kaş): 1984 Campaign. *American Journal of Archaeology* 90(3), pp. 269–296.

Bass, G. F., Lledo, B., Matthews, S., and Brill, R. H. (2009). *Serçe Limani, Vol 2: The Glass of an Eleventh-Century Shipwreck.* College Station: Texas A&M University Press.

Bass, G. F., Pulak, C., Collon, D., and Weinstein, J. (1989). The Bronze Age Shipwreck at Ulu Burun: 1986 Campaign. *American Journal of Archaeology* 93(1), pp. 1–29.

Bass, G. F., Throckmorton, P., Du Plat Taylor, J., et al. (1967). Cape Gelidonya: A Bronze Age Shipwreck. *Transactions of the American Philosophical Society* 57(8), pp. 1–177.

Belfioretti, L. and Vosmer, T. (2010). Al-Balīd Ship Timbers: Preliminary Overview and Comparisons. *Proceedings of the Seminar for Arabian Studies* 40, pp. 111–118.

Bellwood, P. (2004). The Origins and Dispersals of Agricultural Communities in Southeast Asia. In *Southeast Asia: From Prehistory to History*. I. Glover and P. Bellwood, eds. London: Routledge Curzon, pp. 21–40.

Bellwood, P. and Dizon, E. (2005). The Batanes Archaeological Project and the "Out of Taiwan" Hypothesis for Austronesian Dispersal. *Journal of Austronesian Studies* 1(1), pp. 1–31.

Bentley, J. H. (1999). Sea and Ocean Basins as Frameworks of Historical Analysis. *The Geographical Review* 89(2), pp. 215–224.

Blue, L. (2002). Myos Hormos/Quṣeir al-Qadīm: A Roman and Islamic port on the Red Sea coast of Egypt – A maritime perspective. *Proceedings of the Seminar for Arabian Studies* 32, pp. 139–150.

Blue, L. (2006). Sewn Boat Timbers from the Medieval Islamic Port of Quseir al-Qadim on the Red Sea Coast of Egypt. In *Connected by the Sea, Proceedings of the Tenth International Symposium on Boat and Ship Archaeology Roskilde 2003*. L. Blue, F. Hocker, and A. Engler, eds., Oxford: Oxbow Books, pp. 598–610.

Blue, L., Whitewright, J., and Thomas, R. (2011). Ships and Ships' Fittings. In *Myos Hormos – Quseir al-Qadim, Roman and Islamic ports on the Red Sea, Volume 2: Finds from the Excavation 1999–2003*. L. Blue and D. Peacock, eds. Oxford: Archeopress, pp. 179–209.

Bondiolo, M. (2017). Te Libro di navigar, A New Treatise on Venetian Shipbuilding from the 14th Century. In *Ships and Maritime Landscapes: Proceedings of the Thirteenth International Symposium on Boat and Ship Archaeology Amsterdam*. J. Gawronski, A. van Holk, and A. Schokkenbroek, eds. Eelde: Barkhuis.

Braudel, F. (1995). *The Mediterranean and the Mediterranean World in the Age of Philip II*, Siân Reynolds, trans. Berkeley: University of California Press.

Brown, R. M. (2004). History of Shipwreck Excavation in Southeast Asia. In *The Belitung Wreck: Sunken Treasures from Tang China*. J. Ward, Z. Kotitsa, and A. D'Angelo, eds. Nelson: Seabed Explorations, pp. 42–55.

Burge, K. (2021). Queen(s) of the Viking Age. *Agora* 56(1), pp. 27–32.

References

Cai, W., Li C., and Xi, L. (2010). Watertight Bulkheads and Limber Holes in Ancient Chinese Boats. In *Shipwreck Asia*. J. Kimura, ed. Adelaide: Maritime Archaeology Program, Flinders University, pp. 26–31.

Campbell, G. (2019). *Africa and the Indian Ocean World from Early Times to Circa 1900*. Cambridge: Cambridge University Press.

Casson, L. (2014). *Ships and Seamanship in the Ancient World*. Princeton: Princeton University Press.

Castro, F. (2008). In Search of Unique Iberian Ship Design Concepts. *Historical Archaeology* 42(2), pp. 63–87.

Chaudhuri, K. N. (1985). *Trade and Civilization in the Indian Ocean*. Cambridge: Cambridge University Press.

Choksy, J. K. and Nematollahi, N. (2018). The Middle Persian Inscription from a Shipwreck in Thailand: Merchants, Containers, and Commodities. *DABIR* 6(1), pp. 144–150.

Church, Sally K. (2005). Zheng He: An Investigation into the Plausibility of 450-ft Treasure Ships. *Monumenta Serica* 53, pp. 1–43.

Compana, L. (2009). Shipbuilding and Naval Manuscripts from the Venetian Archives, 2007–2009. *Institute of Nautical Archaeology Annual*.

Connan, J., Priestman, S., Vosmer, T., et al. (2020). Geochemical Analysis of Bitumen from West Asian Torpedo Jars from the c. 8th Century Phanom-Surin Shipwreck in Thailand. *Journal of Archaeological Science* 117, pp. 1–18.

Connery, C. (2001). Ideologies of Land and Sea: Alfred Thayer Mahan, Carl Schmitt, and the Shaping of Global Myth Elements. *Boundary 2* 28(2), pp. 13–201.

Connery, C. (2010). Sea Power. *PMLA* 125(3), pp. 685–692.

Crumlin-Pedersen, O. (1990). Boats and Ships of the Angles and Jutes. In *CBA Research Report 71: Maritime Celts, Frisians, and Saxons*. S. McGrail, ed. York: Council for British Archaeology, pp. 98–116.

Crumlin-Pedersen, O. (1997). Large and Small Warships of the North. In *Military Aspects of Scandinavian Society*. Jørgensen, A. N. and Clausen, B. L., eds. Copenhagen: Danish National Museum, pp. 184–194.

Cucchi, T. (2008). Uluburun Shipwreck Stowaway House Mouse: Molar Shape Analysis and Indirect Clues about the Vessel's Last Journey. *Journal of Archaeological Science* 35, pp. 2953–2959.

D'Agostino, M. and Medas, S. (2003). Excavation and Recording of the Medieval Hulls at San Marco in Boccalama (Venice), McManamon J., trans. *The INA Quarterly* 30(1), pp. 22–28.

DAMTCW- Department of Antiquities of the Ministry of Transport, Communications and Works. (2022). *Announcement of the Department of Antiquities on Recent Articles Regarding Shipwrecks in the Sea Zone between*

Cyprus and Lebanon. Nicosia: Press and Information Office, Ministry of Interior, Republic of Cypress.

Dow, G. F. (1927). *Slave Ships and Slaving*. Port Washington: Kennikat Press.

Edgerton, D. (2011). *The Shock of the Old: Technology and Global History since 1900*. Oxford: Oxford University Press.

Edwards, C. R. (1992). The Impact of European Overseas Discoveries on Ship Design and Construction during the Sixteenth Century. *GeoJournal* 26(4), pp. 443–452.

Erickson, N. (2021). The Bellevue Wreck: A Recent Survey of a Large Late Medieval Shipwreck in Dalarö Harbour, Sweden: A Possible Hulk? *International Journal of Nautical Archaeology* 50(1), pp. 116–129.

Ferentinos, G., Fakiris, E., Christodoulou, D., et al. (2020). Optimal Sidescan Sonar and Subbottom Profiler Surveying of Ancient Wrecks: The 'Fiskardo' Wreck, Kefallinia Island, Ionian Sea. *Journal of Archaeological Science* 113, pp. 1–11.

Flecker, M. (2002). *The Archaeological Excavation of the 10th Century Intan Shipwreck*. Oxford: Archaeopress.

Flecker, M. (2010). A Ninth-Century Arab Shipwreck in Indonesia the First Archaeological Evidence of Direct Trade with China. In *Shipwrecked: Tang Treasure and Monsoon Winds*. R. Krahl, J. Guy, J. K. Wilson, and J. Raby, eds. Washington, DC: Smithsonian Institution.

Flexner, J. M. (2021). *Oceania, 800–1800 CE: A Millenium of Interactions in a Sea of Islands*. Cambridge: Cambridge University Press.

Furth, C. (1999). *A Flourishing Yin*. Berkeley: University of California Press.

Gabriele, M. (2021). Vikings, Crusaders, Confederates: Misunderstood Historical Imagery at the January 6 Capitol Insurrection. *Perspectives on History*, January 12.

Garbov, D. and Batchvarov, K. (2022). Served on a Plate: A Late Medieval Ceramic Vessel with Sgraffito Decoration of a Sailing Ship from the Ropotamo Underwater Excavations, Black Sea, Bulgaria. *Heritage* 5(1), pp. 170–191.

Ghidoni, A. (2021). Sewn-plank Construction Techniques in the Western Indian Ocean: Evidence from the Timbers of Al Baleed, Oman. *Archeonautica* 21, pp. 225–232.

Gibb, H. A. R., trans. (1929). *Ibn Battuta: Travels in Asia and Africa, 1325–1354*. London: Routledge.

Gibson-Hill, C. A. (1951). Further Notes on the Old Boat Found at Pontian, in Southern Pahang. *Journal of the Malayan Branch of the Royal Asiatic Society* 25(1), pp. 111–133.

Gilboa, A. and Namdar, D. (2015). On the Beginnings of South Asian Spice Trade with the Mediterranean Region: A Review. *Radiocarbon* 57(2), pp. 265–283.

Gooding, P. (2022). *On the Frontiers of the Indian Ocean World: A History of Lake Tanganyika, c.1830–1890*. Cambridge: Cambridge University Press.

Green, J., Burningham, N., and Museum of Overseas Communication History. (1998). The Ship from Quanzhou, Fujian Province, People's Republic of China. *International Journal of Nautical Archaeology* 27(4), pp. 277–301.

Greenhill, B. (1995). *The Evolution of Sailing Ships 1250–1580; Keynote Studies from the Mariner's Mirror*. London: Conway Maritime Press.

Greenhill, B. and Morrison, J. (1995). *The Archaeology of Boats and Ships: An Introduction*. Annapolis: Naval Institute Press.

The Guardian. (2021). Israeli Archaeologists Find Treasure Trove among Mediterranean Shipwrecks, www.theguardian.com/science/2021/dec/22/israeli-archaeologists-find-treasure-trove-among-mediterranean-shipwrecks.

Guy, J. (2017). The Phanom Surin Shipwreck, a Pahlavi Inscription, and Their Significance for the History of Early Lower Central Thailand. *Journal of the Siam Society* 105, pp. 179–196.

Haw, S. G. (2019). The Genus Afzelia and the Belitung ship. *Journal of the Royal Asiatic Society* 29(3), pp. 1–14.

Heng, D. (2008). Shipping, Customs Procedures, and the Foreign Community: The "Pingzhou ketan" on Aspects of Guangzhou's Maritime Economy in the Late Eleventh Century. *Journal of Song-Yuan Studies* 38, pp. 1–38.

Heng, D. (2019). Southeast Asia-China Economic Interactions in the Late First to Mid-Second Millennium C.E. *Journal of Medieval Worlds* 1(2), pp. 83–92.

Heng, G. (2021). *The Global Middle Ages: An Introduction*. Cambridge: Cambridge University Press.

Heng, D. (2022). *Southeast Asian Interconnections: Geography, Networks, Trade*. Cambridge: Cambridge University Press.

Herodotus. (1921). *The Histories*, Volume II, Godley A. D. trans. Cambridge, MA: Harvard University Press.

Holck, P. (2006). The Oseberg Ship Burial, Norway: New Thoughts on the Skeletons from the Grave Mound. *European Journal of Archaeology* 9(2–3), pp. 185–210.

Horridge, A. (2004). The Austronesian Conquest of the Sea – Upwind. In *The Austronesians: Historical and Comparative Perspectives*. P. Bellwood, J. J. Fox, and D. Tryon, eds. Canberra: ANU Press, pp. 143–160.

Horridge, A. (2008). Origins and Relationships of Pacific Canoes and Rigs. In *Canoes of the Grand Ocean*. A. Di Piazza and E. Pearthree, eds. Oxford: Archeopress, pp. 85–105.

Hough, W. (1893). Time-keeping by Light and Fire. *American Anthropologist* 6(1), pp. 207–210.

Ikeda, Y., Sasaki, R., and Kimura, J. (2019). Recent Underwater Investigations at Takashima. *Current Science* 25(117–10), pp. 1635–1639.

Inglis, D. (2014). The Sea Stories and Stone Sails of Borobudur. In *Proceedings of the 2014 Asia-Pacific Regional Conference on Underwater Cultural Heritage, Session 12: Underwater Cultural Heritage of Southeast Asia*. H. Van Tilburg, S. Tripati, V. Walker, B. Fahy, and J. Kimura, eds. Kingston: URI, The Museum of Underwater Archaeology, pp. 1–14.

Jennings, J. (2010). *Globalizations and the Ancient World*. Cambridge: Cambridge University Press.

Jiao, T. (2021). Archaeology of Southeast China and the Search for an Austronesian Homeland. *Social Sciences in China* 42(1), pp. 161–170.

Jiao, T., Lin, G., and Rolett, B. V. (2002). Early Seafaring in the Taiwan Strait and the Search for Austronesian Origins. *Journal of East Asian Archaeology* 4(1), pp. 307–319.

Jones, Sam. (2023). "A Search for Ourselves": Shipwreck Becomes Focus of Slavery Debate. The Guardian, January 8: www.theguardian.com/environment/2023/jan/08/a-search-for-ourselves-shipwreck-becomes-focus-of-slavery-debate.

Kahanov, Y. (2000). Herodotus 4.42, The Sun Direction. *The Mariner's Mirror* 86(1), pp. 66–72.

Kimura, J. (2016). *Archaeology of East Asian Shipbuilding*. Gainesville: University of Florida Press.

Kirch, P. V. (2017). *On the Road of the Winds: An Archaeological History of the Pacific Islands before European Contact*. Berkeley: University of California Press.

Komoot, A. (2021a). Management of the Phanom-Surin Archaeological Site in Thailand: Concept, Policies and Practices. *International Journal of Asia Pacific Studies* 17(2), pp. 75–105.

Komoot, A. (2021b). *Maritime connections in the Indian Ocean world during the late First Millennium CE: An archaeological study of Phanom-Surin ship in Thailand*. Ph.D. Dissertation. The University of Western Australia.

Krahl, R., Guy, J., and Wilson, J. K., eds. (2010). *Shipwrecked: Tang Treasure and Monsoon Winds*. Washington, DC: Arthur M. Sackler Gallery, Smithsonian Institution.

Kusimba, C. M. (2024). *Swahili Worlds in Globalism*. Cambridge: Cambridge University Press.

Lacsina, L. (2015). The Butuan Boats of the Philippines: Southeast Asian Edge-Joined and Lashed-Lug Watercraft. *Bulletin of the Australasian Institute for Maritime Archaeology* 39, pp. 39–126.

Lansing, J. S., Cox, M. P., de Vet, T. A., et al. (2011). An Ongoing Austronesian Expansion in Island Southeast Asia. *Journal of Anthropological Archaeology* 30, pp. 262–272.

Larsson, A. (2020). Asian Silk in Scandinavian Viking Age Scandinavia. Based on the Boat- and Chamber Graves in Eastern Mälar Valley, Sweden. In *Fragments of Eurasia: Bulletin of the Museum of Far Eastern Antiquities* 81, pp. 107–148.

Lewis, M. E. (2012). *China's Cosmopolitan Empire: The Tang Dynasty*. Cambridge: Belknap Press.

Liang, G. and Wang, F. (2022). Shipwrecks of the Yuan and Ming Dynasties Discovered at Penglai, Yantai, Shandong Province. In *Shipwreck Archaeology in China Sea*. J. Song, ed., *The Archaeology of Asia-Pacific Navigation* 5. Singapore: Springer, pp. 47–73.

Lichtenberg, R. I. and Thuilliez, A. C. (1981). Sur quelques aspects insolites de la radiologie de Ramsès II. *Bulletins et Mémoires de la Société d'anthropologie de Paris* 8(3), pp. 323–330.

Liebner, H. H. (2014). *The Siren of Cirebon: A Tenth-Century Trading Vessel Lost in the Java Sea*. Ph.D. thesis, University of Leeds.

Lo, J. P. (1955). The Emergence of China as a Sea Power during the Late Sung and Early Yuan Periods. *Far Eastern Quarterly* 14(4), pp. 489–503.

Mahan, A. T. (1918). *The Influence of Sea Power upon History, 1660–1783*. Boston: Little Brown.

Mancini, J .M. (2002). Discovering Viking America. *Critical Inquiry* 28(4), pp. 868–890.

Manguin, P. Y. (2012). Southeast Asian Shipping in the Indian Ocean. In *Tradition and Archaeology: Early Maritime Contacts in the Indian Ocean*. H. P. Ray and J. F. Salles, eds. Singapore: Institute of Southeast Asian Studies/Manohar Publishers & Distributors, pp. 181–197.

Manguin, P. Y. (2016). Austronesian Shipping in the Indian Ocean: From Outrigger Boats to Trading Ships. In *Early Exchange between Africa and the Wider Indian Ocean World*. G. Campbell, ed., London: Palgrave, pp. 51–76.

Margaryan, A., D. J. Lawson, M. Sikora et al. (2020). Population Genomics of the Viking World. *Nature* 585, pp. 390–396.

al-Mas'ūdī, 'A. (2020). *Murūj al-Dhahab wa Ma'ādin al-Jawhar*, Vol. 1. Tarif Khalidi, trans. Jerusalem: Khalidi Library.

Mathers, W. M. and Flecker, M. (1997). *Archaeological Recovery of the Java Sea Wreck*. Annapolis: Pacific Sea Resources.

McGrail, S. (2001). *Boats of the World: From the Stone Age to Medieval Times*. Oxford: Oxford University Press.

Miksic, J. (2013). *Singapore and the Silk Road of the Sea: 1300–1800*. Singapore: NUS Press.

Mills, C. W. (2014). *The Racial Contract*. Ithaca: Cornell University Press.

Morton, J. (1992). The Candlenut Tree, Handsome and Wind Resistant, Is a Neglected Ornamental in Florida. *Proceedings of the Florida State Horticultural Society* 105, pp. 251–256.

Needell, C. S. (2018). Cirebon: Islamic Glass from a 10th-Century Shipwreck in the Java Sea. *Journal of Glass Studies* 60, pp. 69–113.

Newson, L. A. (2012). Africans and Luso-Africans in the Portuguese Slave Trade of the Upper Guinea Coast in the Early Seventeenth Century. *Journal of African History* 53, pp. 1–24.

Parry, J. (1951/1952). Ships and Seamen in the Age of Discovery. *Caribbean Quarterly* 2(1), pp. 25–33.

Payton, R. (1991). The Ulu Burun Writing-Board Set. *Anatolian Studies* 41, pp. 99–106.

Pearson, N. (2023). *Belitung: The Afterlives of a Shipwreck*. Honolulu: University of Hawaii Press.

Pearson, R., Li, M., and Li, G. (2002). Quanzhou Archaeology: A Brief Review. *International Journal of Historical Archaeology* 6(1), pp. 23–59.

Plu, A. (1985). Bois et graines. In La momie de Ramsès II. Contribution scientifique à l'égyptologie. L. Balout & C. Roubet, eds. Paris: Éditions Recherches sur les Civilisations, pp. 166–174.

Pomey, P., Kahanov, Y., and Reith, G. (2012). Transition from Shell to Skeleton in Ancient Mediterranean Ship-Construction: Analysis, Problems, and Future Research. *The International Journal of Nautical Archaeology* 41(2), pp. 235–314.

Popovic, A. (1999). *The Revolt of African Slaves in Iraq in the 3rd/9th Century*. Princeton: Markus Wiener.

Pulak, C. (1988). The Bronze Age Shipwreck at Ulu Burun, Turkey: 1985. *American Journal of Archaeology* 92(1), pp. 1–37.

Pulak, C. (1998). The Uluburun Shipwreck: An Overview. *The International Journal of Nautical Archaeology* 27(3), pp. 188–224.

Respess, A. (2020a). *The Abode of Water: Shipwreck Evidence and the Maritime Circulation of Medicine between Iran and China in the 9th through 14th Centuries*. Ph.D. Dissertation. Ann Arbor: The University of Michigan.

Respess, A. (2020b). Islamic Inscriptions on the Belitung Bowls: Ninth-Century Changsha Designs for an Abbasid Market. Paper presented at *China and the Maritime Silk Road: Shipwrecks, Ports, and Products*, Asian Civilisations Museum, Singapore, August 21–23.

Rodríguez-Varela, R., Moore, K. H. S., Ebenesersdóttir, S. S., et al. (2023). The Genetic History of Scandinavia from the Roman Iron Age to the Present. *Cell* 186(1), pp. 32–46.

Jiao, T. L., Lin, T. W., and Rollett, B. (2002). Early Seafaring in the Taiwan Strait and the Search for Austronesian Origins. *Journal of East Asian Archaeology* 4(1), pp. 307–319.

Rolett, B. V., Chen, W. C., and Sinton, J. M. (2000). Taiwan, Neolithic Seafaring and Austronesian Origins. *Antiquity* 74(283), pp. 54–61.

Said, E. W. (1978). *Orientalism*. New York: Pantheon Books.

Samuel, S. (2017). The Strangely Revealing Debate over Viking Couture. *The Atlantic*, October 17. www.theatlantic.com/international/archive/2017/10/viking-couture-allah/543045/.

Schoff, W. H. (1912). *The Periplus of the Erythraean Sea: Travel and Trade in the Indian Ocean by a Merchant of the First Century*. New York: Longmans, Green.

Scott, B. G. (1996). Archaeology and National Identity: The Norwegian Example. *Scandinavian Studies* 68(3), pp. 321–342.

Serva, M. and Pasquini, M. (2022). Linguistic Clues Suggest that the Indonesian Colonizers Directly Sailed to Madagascar. *Language Sciences* 93, 1–11.

Sinvany, B. A. K. (2019). Notes on the Invention of the First Gun: Conflict and Innovation in the Song Warring States Period (960–1279). *Journal of Chinese Military History* 8(2019), pp. 1–28.

al-Sīrāfī, A. Z. (2014). Accounts of China and India, Tim Mackintosh-Smith, trans. In *Two Arabic Travel Books*. New York: New York University Press, pp. vii–161.

Söderström, J. (1938). Notes on Primitive Oil Lamps in the South Seas. *Ethnos* 2(2–3), pp. 64–80.

Steffy, J. R. (1982). Reconstructing the Hull. In *Yassi Ada I*. G. Bass and F. H. van Doornink, eds. College Station: Texas A & M Press, pp. 82–86.

Terrell, J. E. (2009). Reviewed Work(s): From Southeast Asia to the Pacific: Archaeological Perspectives on the Austronesian Expansion and the Lapita Cultural Complex by Scarlett Chiu and Christophe Sand; Oceanic Explorations: Lapita and Western Pacific Settlement by Stuart Bedford, Christophe Sand and Sean P. Connaughton. *Journal of Field Archaeology* 34(3), pp. 364–366.

Trimingham, J. S. (1975). The Arab Geographers and the East African Coast. In *East Africa and the Orient: Cultural Syntheses in Pre-Colonial Times*. H. N. Chittick and R. I. Rottberg, eds. New York: Africana, pp. 115–146.

Tsang, C. H. (2002). Maritime Adaptations in Prehistoric Southeast China: Implications for the Problem of Austronesian Expansion. *Journal of East Asia Archaeology* 3(1), pp. 15–46.

Vedeler, M. (2014). *Silk for the Vikings*. Oxford: Oxbow Books.

Vosmer, T. (2000). Ships in the Ancient Arabian Sea: The Development of a Hypothetical Reed Boat Model. *Proceedings of the Seminar for Arabian Studies, Vol. 30, Papers from the Thirty-Third Meeting of the Seminar for Arabian Studies Held in London*, pp. 235–242.

Wade, G. (2009). An Early Age of Commerce in Southeast Asia, 900–1300 CE. *Journal of Southeast Asian Studies* 40(2), pp. 221–265.

Wärmländer, S. K. T. S., Wåhlander, L., Saage, R., et al. (2015). Analysis and Interpretation of a Unique Arabic Finger Ring from the Viking Town of Birka, Sweden. *Scanning* 37(2), pp. 131–137.

Westerdahl, C. (1995). Society and Sail. In *Ship as Symbol in Prehistoric and Medieval Scandinavia*. O. Crumlin-Pedersen and B. M. Thye, eds. Copenhagen: Danish National Museum, pp. 41–50.

Whitewright, J. (2009). The Mediterranean Lateen Sail in Late Antiquity. *The International Journal of Nautical Archaeology* 38(1), pp. 97–104.

Xi, Chen. (2019). *China's oldest shipwreck reveals secrets of Maritime Silk Road*, www.globaltimes.cn/content/1163040.shtml.

Zhou, Y., Wang, K., Sun, J., Cui, Y., and Hu, D. (2021). Characterizing the Sealing Materials of the Merchant Ship Nanhai I of the Southern Song Dynasty. *Heritage Science* 9(48), pp. 1–10.

Acknowledgements

I would like to express my heartfelt gratitude to Geraldine Heng, Susan Noakes, and Liz Friend-Smith for their extraordinary support in bringing this addition of the Cambridge Elements in the Global Middles Ages to life during a global pandemic. I would also like to thank the students of my 2022 history of global shipbuilding course at The Ohio State University-Marion for their curiosity and candor as I developed this material. Enormous thanks are always due to Lisa C. Niziolek, Chap Kusimba, Gary Feinman, and Jamie Kelly for igniting my own curiosity on global ships at The Field Museum of Natural History many years ago. The research that went into this work would not have been possible without the generous support of The Ohio State University-Marion, the National Science Foundation's Graduate Research Grant No. DGE 1256260, the Boone Scholars Internship Program in East Asian Studies at the Field Museum, the University of Michigan's Institute for Humanities, The Eisenberg Institute for Historical Studies, The University of Michigan's Graduate Program in Museum Studies, The UM Center for the Education of Women, The University of Michigan Joint Program in Anthropology and History, and the Rackham Graduate School. Many thanks to Paula Curtis for her spark and collaboration and Hussein Fancy for his support and guidance in organizing the De-Centering the Global Middle Ages Symposium at the University of Michigan in 2019. I am indebted to the many maritime archaeologists whose work around the globe assembled the material archive this guide is based on, and to the reviewers of this manuscript for their helpful feedback. And, finally, a special thanks to my family for their support while I completed this project.

About the Author

Amanda Respess is Assistant Professor of Premodern World History at The Ohio State University-Marion and holds joint affiliations with The Ohio State University East Asian Studies Center and Middle East Studies Center. She earned a doctorate in Anthropology and History and a Graduate Certificate in Museum Studies at the University of Michigan in 2020 with support from a Graduate Research Fellowship from the National Science Foundation. She has conducted collections research and field work in China, Singapore, the United Kingdom, and the United States. She began over a decade of research on the premodern shipwrecks of the spice routes as a Boone Scholar Research Intern in the Anthropology Department of the Field Museum of Natural History in Chicago, where she conducted extensive collections research on the cargo of the Java Sea Shipwreck.

Cambridge Elements ≡

The Global Middle Ages

Geraldine Heng
University of Texas at Austin

Geraldine Heng is Perceval Professor of English and Comparative Literature at the University of Texas, Austin. She is the author of *The Invention of Race in the European Middle Ages* (2018) and *England and the Jews: How Religion and Violence Created the First Racial State in the West* (2018), both published by Cambridge University Press, as well as *Empire of Magic: Medieval Romance and the Politics of Cultural Fantasy* (2003, Columbia). She is the editor of *Teaching the Global Middle Ages* (2022, MLA), coedits the University of Pennsylvania Press series, RaceB4Race: Critical Studies of the Premodern, and is working on a new book, Early Globalisms: The Interconnected World, 500–1500 CE. Originally from Singapore, Heng is a Fellow of the Medieval Academy of America, a member of the Medievalists of Color, and Founder and Co-director, with Susan Noakes, of the Global Middle Ages Project: www.globalmiddleages.org.

Susan J. Noakes
University of Minnesota–Twin Cities

Susan J. Noakes is Professor of French and Italian at the University of Minnesota–Twin Cities, where she also serves as Chair of the Department of French and Italian. For her many publications in French, Italian, and comparative literature, the university in 2009 named her Inaugural Chair in Arts, Design, and Humanities. Her most recent publication is an analysis of Salim Bachi's *L'Exil d'Ovide*, exploring a contemporary writer's reflection on his exile to Europe by comparing it to Ovid's exile to the Black Sea; it appears in *Salim Bachi*, edited by Agnes Schaffhauser, published in Paris by Harmattan in 2020.

Lynn Ramey
Vanderbilt University

Lynn Ramey is Professor of French and Cinema and Media Arts at Vanderbilt University and Chair of the Department of French and Italian. She is the author of *Jean Bodel: An Introduction* (2024, University Press of Florida), *Black Legacies: Race and the European Middle Ages* (2014, University Press of Florida), and *Christian, Saracen and Genre in Medieval French Literature* (2001, Routledge). She is currently working on recreations of medieval language, literature, and culture in video games for which she was awarded an NEH digital humanities advancement grant in 2022.

About the Series

Elements in the Global Middle Ages is a series of concise studies that introduce researchers and instructors to an uncentered, interconnected world, c. 500–1500 CE. Individual Elements focus on the globe's geographic zones, its natural and built environments, its cultures, societies, arts, technologies, peoples, ecosystems, and lifeworlds.

Cambridge Elements

The Global Middle Ages

Elements in the Series

Cahokia and the North American Worlds
Sarah E. Baires

Eurasian Musical Journeys: Five Tales
Gabriela Currie and Lars Christensen

Global Medievalism: An Introduction
Helen Young and Kavita Mudan Finn

Southeast Asian Interconnections: Geography, Networks and Trade
Derek Heng

Slavery in East Asia
Don J. Wyatt

Late Tang China and the World, 750–907 CE
Shao-yun Yang

Early Tang China and the World, 618–750 CE
Shao-yun Yang

Medieval Textiles across Eurasia, c. 300–1400
Patricia Blessing, Elizabeth Dospěl Williams and Eiren L. Shea

The Chertsey Tiles, the Crusades, and Global Textile Motifs
Amanda Luyster

Swahili Worlds in Globalism
Chapurukha M. Kusimba

"Ethiopia" and the World, 330–1500 CE
Yonatan Binyam and Verena Krebs

Global Ships: Seafaring, Shipwrecks, and Boatbuilding in the Global Middle Ages
Amanda Respess

A full series listing is available at: www.cambridge.org/EGMA

For EU product safety concerns, contact us at Calle de José Abascal, 56–1°,
28003 Madrid, Spain or eugpsr@cambridge.org.